Wounded Leaders:

How Their Damaged Past Affects Your Future

By

Allan Bonner, BA, BEAD, MA,
MSc, DBA, LLM, MScPl (Cand.)

Wounded Leaders: How Their Damaged Past Affects Your Future

First printing, June, 2014

Published by Sextant Publishing, Edmonton, Alberta, Canada

Printed in Canada by Thistle Printing Limited, Toronto, Ontario, Canada

Book Design and Layout by Dean Pickup, CanadaBookDesign.com

ISBN: 978-1-926755-05-2

For educational or institutional discounts or for information about seminars and speeches, please contact:

Sextant Publishing, Edmonton, Alberta, Canada
or
www.allanbonner.com
Toll-free phone: 1-877-484-1667

THE COVER:
St. Sebastian is one of the saints most frequently used as subjects by artists through the centuries. Here he is depicted in his martyrdom by artist Gerrit van Honthorst (1623). According to his legend, Sebastian was a captain in the Praetorian Guard, and an early Christian leader in the third century. Having converted prisoners to Christianity, he was sentenced to death by the Emperor Diocletian. This was carried out by tying him to a tree and shooting him with arrows. He reportedly survived the ordeal (perhaps by divine intervention) and used the opportunity to return to Diocletian and harangue him about the persecution of Christians. The Emperor again sentenced him to death, and he was beaten to death with clubs.

Praise for
Allan Bonner's
Wounded Leaders

Good leadership is the glue that bonds a successful organization into a cohesive whole, from top to bottom. And good leadership, as capably described by Allan Bonner in this book, is not something that you're born with; it is a quality that successful leaders–civilian and military -have learned, developed, nurtured and applied to the best advantage and to the betterment of the organizations to which they have dedicated themselves. Those who would aspire to become capable and respected leaders have much to learn from those who have succeeded, but they also have much to learn from this book. In particular, they will benefit significantly from the wise counsel that it offers on various types of leadership and the weight of importance that it gives to listening as well as providing guidance and positive influence. Indeed, and in my experience, the best leaders are those that have mastered the art of communication–both ways.

Ray Henault

Gen (Ret'd)
Former Chief of the Defence Staff, and
Former Chairman of the NATO Military Committee

---

*"Forceful, insightful and practical ...
and, on top of that, a very good read."*

Aram Bakshian, Jr.,

Founding Editor of American Speaker and Director of
Presidential Speech-writing for Ronald Reagan

"...Allan Bonner applies a lifetime of astute observation, involvement, and critical, scholarly thinking to the very practical matter of why businesses fail to meet their goals."

Dr. Joseph C. Braun

Argonne Nuclear laboratory

"The amalgamation of modern western psychology and ancient eastern martial arts philosophy has been the cornerstone of the curriculum I have promoted for many years. Again I turn with special trust and confidence to Dr. Allan Bonner and this, his latest work, which will serve as an inspiration to me, and an instalment to my own research and reference library."

Detective James Shanahan

Police Academy City of New York

"Is morality a necessary part of leadership? Should a leader be hard-driving? With more and more regions and countries joining the still evolving global market...the rules will change."

Rodney Moore

Former External Affairs speech-writing Attaché, as well as Press Secretary, to Governors-General Michener and Léger at Government house, Ottawa; then Assistant Press Secretary to The Queen at Buckingham Palace (1974-1977), at the same time also Press Secretary to The Duke of Edinburgh, The Prince of Wales and The Princess Anne; later Political Counsellor at the Canadian Embassy, Saudi Arabia; and Official Spokesperson for the Canadian Embassy, Washington, covering the 9/11 period.

Also by the author:

Doing and Saying the Right Thing
Professional Risk and Crisis Management

Media Relations

Political Conventions
The Art of Getting Elected and Governing

Speaking, Writing and Presenting in SOCKOs®
Strategic Overriding Communications & Knowledge Objectives

Political Columns
Behind the Scenes with Powerful People

Tough Love at the Table
Power, Culture and Diversity in Negotiations, Mediation and Conflict Resolution

FOREWORD

I came to know Allan Bonner through a series of training courses that the International Atomic Energy Agency (IAEA) conducts around the world to help promote the safety and good management of nuclear power plants and nuclear facilities. I have organized a number of these courses at the Argonne National Laboratory located near Chicago, Illinois in the U.S.A. Allan has lectured in many of these courses, and I had come to look forward to his exciting and dynamic presentations on the importance of good facility management and the need for developing good relations with the public–especially people who live in the vicinity of these large plants. When he told me that he was working on a new book on the topic of leadership, I immediately asked to see an advanced copy, hoping that it would lead to new lectures by him.

I have read other books by Allan Bonner, and they are all written in a crisp, succinct style that drives home a sequence of thoughts, ideas and concepts, in a manner not unlike the SOCKO© method that he advocates. Bonner likes to select a bite-sized topic and present it with both scholarship and style in a way that it is both enjoyable and memorable. In his new book, Wounded Leaders, he uses this writing style to identify a serious and growing problem that is plaguing the world of business.

There are many books today that talk about success in business. Bonner has chosen to approach this topic through the 'back door' and talk rather about the epidemic of failures–sometimes catastrophic–that we have seen in the recent recession and which continue to the present. We tend to ascribe much of the credit (or blame) for a company's success (or failure) to the goals, strategies, tactics and style employed by the company leaders.

Regarding failures or lacklustre performance, he asks, "Why do so many business leaders fail to recognize the danger signs that prevent them from reaching their full personal and corporate potential?" In this book he whisks through an extensive list of findings and examples that he learned of while conducting his doctoral research on the topic of leadership. He offers a number of cases and vignettes that might explain the shortcomings of corporate leadership. Several of these stand out–the case of the wounded child who eventually becomes a wounded leader who goes on to head the wounded organization. Much wasted time, energy, inefficiency, and loss of productivity, stems from these wounded leaders. In searching for the roots of these problems, Bonner finds a shocking lack of traditional values: hard work, short turnaround times, respect for tradition and rank, humility, clean simple living, and an old term that has taken on a new meaning–followership–the capacity to learn from others.

Bonner seeks to find a model organization, that works well and implements the traditional values that he cherishes. But where does one find such an organization?

Surprisingly, Bonner finds such an organization right under his nose. For years he has practiced Karate as a physical and psychological diversion from his workplace. He ponders the problems of corporate management on his way to and from his Karate Dojo. Finally it strikes him that a well-run Karate Dojo has all of the good qualities that he would like to see in a well-run business organization. A significant portion of the book makes these comparisons and shows how respect for others, practise, learning and training, a constant striving for excellence and a high level of performance, along with a sprinkling of tradition and ritual, mark the attributes of some of the world's best run and most successful organizations.

Finally, Bonner adds a set of appendices that offer help for the wounded leader through a "twelve-step" program, a list of principles and practices that connect life in a Dojo to the world of business, and a list of personal insights, observations and wisdom that can be helpful in the world of business.

In this book Allan Bonner applies a lifetime of astute observation, involvement, and critical, scholarly thinking to the very practical matter of why businesses fail to meet their goals. This new approach to an age-old problem may be the starting point of a whole new way of looking at and improving the management systems that we all depend on to run our modern organizations.

JCB

Joseph C. Braun Ph.D.
Nuclear Engineer
Nuclear Engineering Division
Argonne National Laboratory

INDEX

ACKNOWLEDGEMENTS

It's always tempting to reveal some insight, or gossip, about the difficulties and joys of research and writing. I try to reserve the joy for myself and delegate the difficulties to others. But, more seriously, the others deserve thanks.

I've always found the thanks to wives in introductions a little pro forma. I'd like to rise above that. The best way I can describe Lorna Jackson's input is as a professional writer, broadcaster, researcher and reader. Lorna began her career as a researcher for the landmark CBC TV shows "Marketplace" and "Take 30". I benefit from her skills most days as she sends me links to things I'm studying or writing about. In this case, she suggested using the image of St. Sebastian to symbolize the wounded leader. She also read several drafts of my Doctoral thesis on which this book is based and then read this draft several times. Lorna's quiet input and encouragement takes her away from her own projects and I'm grateful.

My boys, grown men now, have made sacrifices and

contributions too. I interrupted many vacations with work. They saw many kitchen and dining room tables strewn with papers. But then the tables turned. Both Michael and Christian began carving out their own areas of interest and were able to add something new to mine. Michael's knowledge of languages and history and Christian's of music, popular culture and mythology have enriched my understanding. Michael has helped me parse words by knowing their roots and manifestations in other languages, and Christian added the concept of the "wounded king". I am enjoying speaking with both as men now.

I lucked out with a great supervisor for my Doctorate–Dr. Roy Damary, Oxonian, Harvardian, lay preacher and entrepreneur. Roy is the author of an economic newsletter that warns of trouble years before it happens and has become a great friend. I've visited him in Geneva and he's visited me in Toronto. We've travelled in Europe and North America together. I continue to rely on his guidance. At one point in my writing my 85,000 word Dissertation for Roy, he said it appeared I was trying to codify every life experience I'd ever had. This was not far off the mark. I drew on my consulting practice with leaders, quantitative research with a large sample group, reflections of the trainers in my company, academic study and my experiences being coached. I thought it was thorough and panoptic, but it could also have been termed a mish-mash.

This is where Editor Hal Jones came in. Years after my Doctorate was accepted, it came time to turn the material into an accessible book for leaders and those who work with leaders— and that's just about everybody. I'm lucky to have had Hal in my company for about 15 years. We had been on the same newscasts—me from Toronto and he from London, Washington and

Moscow for some years, but had never met face to face until I'd left Canada's national public broadcaster–CBC, and he was on the verge of leaving. Hal observed leaders from his posts abroad. The leaders included four US Presidents and many Eastern European leaders during the dying days of the Soviet Union.

I often describe Hal's skill to clients with an anecdote. I point out that for 18 years, mainly during the Cold War, Hal had to delve through a stack of material each day in London, Moscow and Washington. It was a mixture of news reports, official and unofficial press releases, background papers, analysis, etc., about what went on in the White House, State Department, Pentagon, No. 10 Downing Street, the Foreign Office, NATO and the Kremlin. Hal had to decide, on deadline, what was news, what was propaganda and what was just the usual detritus of bureaucracy. He got it right, including when time zones caused his deadline to be 3:00 a.m. on a regular basis. So, when Hal has to work on the weekends for one of our clients it's an easy day–no overnights, no gunfire and no long flights to the Middle East. My giving Hal my 85,000 precious academic words and asking him to translate it into more accessible language was just another day at the office. Hal has a remarkable skill in finding the coherent thread, entry point (or lead) and pulling diverse thoughts together. We've had a good run and great second careers thanks to Hal.

And this brings me to the literature search. There are two schools of thought in the academic world. One is that a literature search should stand alone, showing a comprehensive attempt to understand research and writing on the topic that has gone before. The assumption is that new work is anchored in and a reflection of the old. The other school is that new ideas and research should have woven into them citations and references to existing scholarship. I've done both, taught both and have had supervising professors with both preferences.

As this thesis became a book, two things became clear. The stand-alone literature search felt like a gigantic pause in the narrative, lasting about a third of the book. There was no logical flow in the narrative. In fact, the flow stopped while countless studies and authors were summarized. Weaving in the citations kept a flow of sorts, but still slowed things down. We had to have a compromise between the ethics of citations and the accessibility of the material.

In the academic environment, I've always been a stickler for citations. Many use the term "paradigm" without reference to Thomas Kuhn or "sustainability" without crediting Madam Brundtland. Some argue these terms have become part of common parlance. Perhaps, but there is a difference between dinner party conversation and an academic paper. Footnotes may get edited out at dinner, but not in the classroom.

Then there's this book. What to do? Hal's advice was to achieve a smooth flow of information, uninterrupted by footnotes, quotes and in-text references. My instinct was to reference. But, I also remembered instruction from undergraduate days to put more than six words from another source in quotation marks and cite. The same Professor, instructing young students who were worried about form and format issues, said that a citation in the bibliography was the minimum standard.

So, you'll see a bit of a contradiction in this manuscript. There is a lengthy bibliography and I'm grateful to the authors cited. But, there are few citations in the text. That doesn't mean the text doesn't draw on the bibliography–it does in many substantial ways. I've rationalized this compromise in several ways.

First, it will be pretty obvious that my "wounded leader" draws on titles that reference narcissism, working yourself to death, mental illness, good companies going bad, self-destruction, chaos, fear, humility and so on. The references to mergers and acquisitions and various books on leadership are also self-explanatory.

The ethnographic literature is there to anchor my work in a 150-year-old tradition of examination of the human condition in the field. "SCSPO" is a reference to the Scarman Centre for the Study of Public Order at Leicester University–the most remarkable and valuable academic program I've attended.

The references to Jack Welch draw on the citations with his name, but mainly on John Cassidy's work. It will be pretty easy to see that I obtained statistics on the cost of depression from articles that reference this topic in their titles. Terrance Real deserved an in-text reference because of his "wounded child" concept. The crisis literature is there because it's in crisis that I often coach leaders and it's in a crisis when leadership traits are writ large.

The Eastern and Martial literature has obviously informed my personal experience in a Karate Dojo. This is also the case with the general business literature on decision making and organizational matters. It should be obvious that I'm grateful for my time studying leadership at Harvard and to the Harvard Business Review for easy to access compilations on topic of importance to my work and that's why the HBR appears so often.

I hope that's credit where it's due. Errors and omissions are mine.

INTRODUCTION

The western world is in danger of being failed by its corporate leaders. That's a sweeping statement to make, but the evidence is piling up. In fact, it was distressingly apparent even before the body blows that rocked the world economy beginning in 2007-8. Leadership failures had already been a hot topic in academic literature and the business media for a decade. For decades before that researchers studied the waste and financial failure of mergers and acquisitions. Unfortunately nobody seems to be listening. There's very little sign of change in the mindset and approach of those who lead the corporate world.

I studied the strengths, weaknesses and foibles of the corporate world for my doctoral thesis in 2005. What I found becomes more relevant with each failure and headline. The economic meltdown sparked by the sub-prime mortgage debacle in the US changed lives around the world but it has not prevented corporate leaders from continuing to endanger their business organizations by failing to learn from the past.

Why? Why do so many business leaders fail to recognize the danger signs that prevent them from reaching their full personal and corporate potential?

There are a number of possible explanations. One is the complexity of modern business organizations. Leaders must operate within a labyrinth of trade pacts, labour agreements, jurisdictional and financial regulations as well as the ups and downs of the business cycle. All this may well result in modern leaders having less influence on their business organizations than their predecessors enjoyed. Business life was simpler for the men (they were mostly men) who laid the foundations of the modern industrial state during the late 19th and early part of the 20th centuries.

Ours is a very different world. Just think of air travel, e-commerce and instant communication. And there were more developments, twists and turns during the more than three years I spent researching this book. In the wake of the sub-prime and other financial scandals, we've seen a sharp rise in criticism of Big Business and Big Banks and the way they use trade and tax rules to maximize profits and minimize taxes. The Occupy Movement was one of the most obvious–and least focused– manifestations of this anti-business backlash. But there's also been a much more focused response.

In 2013, governments of the world's 20 largest economies (the G20) and countries of the Organisation for Economic and Co-operation Development (OECD) began looking at what was termed the "Base-Erosion and Profit-Sharing" (BEPS) issue. This project took me to Washington to see first-hand how the world was going to deal with funding the 40% of the OECD economies that are public sector, while their tax bases are being eroded because Big Business is contributing less and less to tax coffers. My clients wanted to make their case to the OECD and G20.

At about the same time, The Public Accounts Committee of the British House of Commons held public hearings in which the politicians castigated Google, Starbucks, Amazon as well as their own government's tax collectors. They also grilled the "Big Four" accounting firms–PwC, KPMG, Deloitte, and, Ernst & Young. At issue is whether these international corporations were paying their "fair share" of taxes. They are operating in countries with bilateral and multilateral trade agreements, as well as within large trading blocks with additional rules. The system set out in 1927 by the long-defunct League of Nations is just not up to dealing with modern commerce.

When average people hear that Starbucks paid little or no tax in England for many years, they naturally wonder. But in our modern, highly-mobile world, assessing taxes due is complex. How much credit do the people who started the company in Seattle get? How much does the grower, the buyer, grinder and shipper get? What about the person who devises the logo, designs the stores and the inventor of the machinery that makes the coffee and keeps it hot? Have all these people made their contribution or is it just the server behind the counter in London or Manchester who pours hot water over the ground beans?

The lesson for leaders was stark during these times. I watched with some horror at the poor performance of every senior spokesperson who appeared before the Public Accounts Committee in London. Each struggled to explain the difference between tax evasion and tax avoidance. Each struggled to defend the practice of "transfer pricing" the accounting method used by many multinationals to apportion taxable values. They were accused of unethical behaviour and didn't seem able to defend themselves.

Testimony went better for Apple in Washington, but the message was clear. Business leaders are not dictators. They need "permission to do business" from regulators, legislators and the public. In the changed business climate since 2007, they are not given the benefit of the doubt or the "elbow room" they need to lead. Why? What is wrong with the reputation of our leaders and why are they under such suspicion?

Another failure is the widespread reliance on military-style jargon, bullet point presentations, hollow headlines and slo-gans to convey information to colleagues and employees instead of clear, unambiguous language. Too many leaders are under the impression they need to use important-sounding language to convey authority. They're wrong. It may work in the board-room with subordinates nodding "yes", but it doesn't work in the rough and tumble of a legislative committee or in the media.

A third involves a personality disorder, which I call *the wounded leader*. It describes a swashbuckling, hard-driving male executive who often harms himself, his colleagues and even his organization in his zeal to prove his qualifications to lead. One of the easiest ways to harm a corporate entity or organization is for its leader to assume the authority he exercises in his busi-ness life also extends to public officials and those affected by his organization's activities.

Three highly publicized oil spills in North America are linked not just by the damage they did, but by the inept behaviour and comments of the top dogs of the companies responsible. These are: the oil spills from the grounded super tanker *Exxon Valdez* off Alaska in 1989, the 2010 explosion at BP's *Deepwater Horizon* oil rig in the Gulf of Mexico in 2010 and the derailment and explosion of oil tanker cars in Lac-Megantic, Quebec in 2013. The names of Lawrence Rawl, CEO of Exxon; Tony Hayward, CEO of BP; and Ed Burkhardt, Chairman of Montreal, Maine and Atlantic Railway will forever be linked to these disasters because of their ill-considered comments and combative attitudes.

In my years as a journalist, I was struck by just how few senior people, in either the private or public sector, had a clear message or command of relevant issues and facts pertaining to their own organizations. Later, as a coach and trainer of politicians and corporate leaders, I watched senior spokespeople under real-time pressure struggling to decide, motivate and communicate. Many arrived for training sessions in crisis management and communications unprepared and unwilling to learn.

The world, social behaviour, methods of communication and the entire financial climate have changed over the last 30 years. Top business leaders talk about change all the time but seem unable or unwilling to change the way they lead.

I'm convinced this situation is a crisis in management and leadership, robbing the economy of much needed wealth and productivity.

In spite of ample evidence that three-quarters of all mergers and acquisitions are failures, CEOs and their boards of directors persist in chasing this discredited dream. And this is only one symptom of the crisis in our corporate leadership. For years the business and other media (and even Hollywood!) have drawn attention to questionable ethical and moral behaviour of corporate leaders, especially when their organizations get into trouble. In recent years corporate leaders have been criticized for awarding themselves multimillion dollar bonuses, taking advantage of expensive perks such as corporate jets and claiming huge "golden handshakes" or retirement packages even while their company shares are plummeting.

There has to be a better way. We in the West have become so accustomed to thinking that we lead the world in technical and business know-how that we are reluctant to look beyond our horizons for something better. My search for proven styles of leadership in other fields led me to study the leadership used in a Karate school, or Dojo. There I found several concepts, which–I believe–could benefit modern business organizations. These include hard work, short turnaround times, respect for tradition, rank, ritual, and what can be termed *followership*–the capacity to learn from others. Leaders need to be able to relinquish their roles to allow followers to take over if they are better able to accomplish the task.

Of course respect for tradition, rank and ritual may seem contrary to the egalitarian principles our Western societies have tried to encourage during the last half-century. These and some other aspects may not translate well into modern corporate life. But I suggest that many concepts of the Dojo, including *followership*, skills development, the episodic nature of leadership, and short bursts of hard work can benefit our business organizations.

Another important prescription for more efficient leadership is empathy. Psychologists note those who seek and achieve high office and positions of power often display a bombastic and bullying nature, which masks fear and hurt. Academic literature, my practice and my observations of leaders and executives working under pressure suggest that wellness begins with empathy. There must be empathy for one's self before there can be empathy for others or one's organization.

This book examines how today's troubled corporate culture came about, how bad a crisis it really is and how to address the leadership challenges it poses.

THE PROBLEM

Stories about the challenges of corporate leadership in the areas of ethics, human relations and profitability have dominated the business and academic press for thirty years. Corporate officers are in jail. Pension funds have been raided. The lavish personal spending of even the most revered CEOs has come under shareholder and media scrutiny. There has been a flurry of mergers and acquisitions during the period designed to produce "synergies", "convergence" and economies of scale. Corporate restructuring has coincided with "outsourcing" to low-wage developing countries and downsizing among the Fortune 500.

In the Western democracies, education is often cited as the panacea for a wide range of troubles. Yet, ironically, corporate leadership and performance troubles seem to have become more pronounced as education levels have risen. Leadership challenges have multiplied despite a rise in the number of graduates of business schools and other faculties in the workforce.

1

Why do corporate leaders rise to the top and then, so often, fail in such spectacular ways? They misread markets and misunderstand cultures, causing not only the collapse of transnational expansion plans, but also high turnover rates and poor financial performance. Some engage in illegal activities.

There is a personal and organizational toll being paid for these failures. In the same way that the modern executive pushes the organization with downsizing, attacking new markets, mergers and acquisitions, the executive pushes himself or herself. Men seem to be more susceptible, but women are not immune to this personal toll.

In recent years our "advanced" societies have realized there is also an economic cost to this destructive behaviour with impacts felt far beyond the workplace and have begun to assess the damage. Mental disorders are exacting a very high toll in reduced economic productivity, medical treatment and social assistance.

As reported by Canada's *Globe and Mail* (10.13.2013): "In fact, it is estimated that mental illness costs the economy more than $50-billion a year." One of the reasons that number is so high is because problems are so widespread–an estimated 6.7 million Canadians suffer from mental illness–"*and illness tends to hit people hardest in their prime work years.*" (Emphasis added).

One estimate for the United States is that about 15 million Americans will suffer from depression in a given year and that more than 35 million will experience a major depressive episode at some point in their lives. The economic cost is estimated to be approaching $100 billion–and depression is only one of several mental disorders. There are also costs associated with heart disease, diabetes, marital breakdown and other problems.

So what is it that modern leaders think they are achieving by the sacrifices they demand of themselves, the people around them and their organizations? What do they think they are achieving for their organizations with countless rounds of unproductive mergers and acquisitions? Is it inertia? Is it to fill time or put their marks on organizations? Do they think they must "get the job done" at any price, including their own health? With downsizing, failed mergers and so on, is it a case of "this hurts me more than you"?

The statistics on corporate failure are only representative of the human condition. These failures represent lost jobs, lost shareholder value, less pension money for retirees and perhaps even shorter lives. In turn, the children of workers, shareholders and retirees may be paying a price in lost educational opportunities, poor diet and fewer life experiences. In the modern global economy, there are no bystanders any more.

People at all levels of corporations and society are paying a price for these failures. Workers and pensioners are obvious examples, but so are the leaders and their colleagues who are often painted as the authors of these organizational failings. Obesity and hypertension are on the increase, and even appear to be a rite of passage to the executive suite. One quotation, perhaps apocryphal, but that circulates among executives I've studied, has a famous CEO saying that if you have not had a heart attack by age fifty-five, you are not working hard enough. Those senior executives who seem to escape physical ailments often seek counselling for psychological support. Still others cannot keep marriages and families together while pursuing corporate goals.

It is ironic that these days almost any discussion or

examination of modern corporate life is dominated by the challenges and failures of today's leaders. The very word "leadership" conjures images of big, larger-than-life personalities who can be role models for the rest of us. Think of Churchill, de Gaulle, Reagan, Thatcher or Trudeau. Whom we choose as our models depends on our origins, culture, perspective and beliefs.

In North America, any list of business leaders is dominated by names from the US. Historically, these would likely include Rockefeller, Carnegie, Morgan, Whitney and Ford. We tend to think of these men as decisive, ethical, hard working, strong, competent, single-minded—and also excellent communicators. However, we also know that history is written by the "victors" and while their biographers may have been frank and fair we have to concede these men had an easier time of it than today's captains of industry. It's easier to exercise and project power when you have time to write a speech, or react to bad news when there's no television or internet demanding instant answers and solutions—and analyzing what you've said before you've even finished speaking.

The odd thing is that even though today's leaders live and work in a totally different world from their business ancestors, they persist in chasing the same old dream: bigger is better. Of course there's nothing wrong with making more cars or widgets, if that is your core business. However, a widget maker who wants to generate more profits by taking over a very successful ice cream business based in a different country is likely to find he's bitten off more than he can chew, lick, or swallow. And far too often our business leaders over the past three decades have chosen the latter option in the race to grow bigger, better—and richer.

The Magnetism of Mergers and Acquisitions

There are numerous aspects of organizational life that could be studied as manifestations of the health of the modern corporation. We might examine recent accounting and ethical wrongdoing and come to the conclusion that there's been a failure to instill in young people a code of good business conduct. We could also study extreme examples of executive compensation and attempt to link that phenomenon to the evolution of our consumer society. An anthropologist might even relate high executive compensation to conspicuous consumption. Indeed, there could be a long list of potentially fruitful areas of inquiry to explain selected aspects of organizational life.

Mergers and acquisitions present a particularly useful approach to the study of the effects of leaders' behaviour. Many organizations have channelled significant energy–and resources–into these activities in the past thirty years. In addition, this is an area that has been the subject of many academic and business studies–and the evidence all points in one direction. Mergers and acquisitions rarely produce the benefits expected of them. So why have they been so popular? What is it that makes leaders risk so much when the odds are against them and the dangers so obvious?

The business press often has featured headlines about mergers and acquisitions as if they were trumpeting Allied victories in World War II or great advances in medical science. The economic story under those headlines, however, tells a much different tale. Staggeringly, three quarters of all mergers and acquisitions fail to meet their hoped-for goals.

One reason is the inability to know all there is to know about the company being acquired or with which one is merging. In addition to facilities, people, inventory, products, technology and other assets, you may be buying a lot of problems. One case study I came across of an ad hoc method of developing a security system in a large corporation can serve as a metaphor for how mergers and acquisitions may proceed:

> "How does management proceed? Usually piecemeal. First, a security officer (probably unqualified) is hired, followed by an alarm company together, perhaps, with guards and gatekeepers. No attempt is made to make an independent assessment of the risk—present and future—and then construct an appropriate plan based on that assessment, available resources and vulnerability...."
>
> (Hamilton, P., The Administration of Corporate Security and Crime Prevention. 1 [1], 1987, 11-19.)

In the world of mergers and acquisitions, the parallel to this uncharitable account would be that management would proceed from an assumption that mergers and acquisitions are a necessary activity without first conducting the assessment of risk and rewards. It's the cart before the horse.

Among the problems being purchased in mergers and acquisitions are those under the heading of cultural differences. This can mean the need to overcome language, religious and other barriers that are often associated with national boundaries. The challenge of doing business in Japan is the oft-cited example of dealing with unfathomable cultural differences. However, there can also be considerable cultural differences in countries that seem much closer. Germany and America are allies, trading partners and both are major industrial nations producing high quality automobiles. However, the Daimler Chrysler merger shows that even these common traits may not bridge cultural differences.

Even with a common language, as in America and England, there can be large cultural problems. In fact it is also possible to find cultural differences in the same industry and in the same community.

Culture has to do with nations, religions, languages and ethnicity, but it is also a collection of beliefs, norms, attitudes, roles and practices of a given group, organization, institution or society which is highly resistant to change. However it would be wrong to conclude that cultural matters are the only cause of failure when organizations attempt to merge.

Problems can also become evident in human resource matters. Productivity is known to decline during all periods of turmoil and uncertainty in corporate life. An organization may lose staff, and productivity may fall to less than an hour per day. Moreover, these human resource challenges may not fade after the merger is complete. The effects of the turmoil that mergers and acquisitions bring to long-term productivity, loyalty, morale and access to skilled workers may be profound.

There are also less visible or obvious dangers in mergers and acquisitions. As in biological mergers, business mergers can transmit dormant ailments. The metaphor in the era of safe sex is that one is having intercourse with every partner one's partner has ever had. The metaphor may seem dramatic, but in the corporate context it is essential that the acquiring entity knows about any potential liabilities–such as environmental exposures, retiree health-care liabilities or legal actions for which it is assuming responsibility.

An example is the Bridgestone Company's acquisition of Firestone. Bridgestone not only purchased inventory, a sales network, factories and a well-known brand name, but also the Firestone history. In that history are acrimonious labour relations, the largest tire recall in history, reluctance to embrace radial technology, questionable methods of storing raw materials, a questionable vulcanizing process and a relationship by marriage to the Ford family. So it should not have been surprising when a scandal, lawsuits and an even larger tire recall hit the new company. Certainly, the Japanese parent company had to grapple with US culture and the Ford relationship, which it did not do easily.

Perhaps the most damning of all evidence against mergers and acquisitions can be found on the balance sheet. Acquirers often overpay for target companies. The most notorious example may be Quaker Oats' purchase of Snapple soft drinks in 1994. In that acquisition, the $1.7 billion purchase price eventually was judged as being $1 billion too much. In 1997 Quaker sold the brand for less than 20% of the purchase price.

Research has shown that a majority of M & A deals destroy value for the acquiring company's shareholders. Returns for at least 71% of those deals are negative in the year following the merger.

As in human relations, foibles can be a root cause of unproductive and even destructive behaviour. Wishful thinking, a lack of unique offerings and a lack of rigorous assessment of the potential can all play a role in unproductive mergers and acquisitions. Some leaders may need to prove their worth to themselves and others. They may also crave the feeling or "high" that frenetic activity brings. It's known that emotion and ego play large roles in both personal and professional failure. But there is also a financial manifestation to that failure.

A major bank studied the three decade frenzy of buying that ended at the turn of the century. It revealed that companies throughout the world spent "$3.3 trillion on mergers and acquisitions in 1999–fully 32% more than was spent in 1998. This resulted in a failure to realize expected gains from a whopping $1.6 trillion in investments". Ironically, almost the entire thirty-year period of buying and merging repeatedly failed to achieve desired results.

Not surprisingly, business academics and others have enjoyed a field day speculating on why leaders engage in such unproductive activity and why organizations fail to realize their full potential. A lack of effective response to the business environment is one of the most perplexing aspects of organizational behaviour, says one study in the bibliography at the end of this book. Another blames gargantuan egos for causing the demise or continued mediocrity of companies in two-thirds of the cases studied. One author wonders whether some are compensating for dark and complex reasons rooted in childhood trauma!

It could be that mergers and acquisitions simply appear to be the appropriate way of doing business. Belief in an ever-expanding economy seems to point to the imperative of continuous growth. If new markets and products do not manifest themselves easily from the marketing and production departments, mergers and acquisitions may seem to be the appropriate means of achieving growth.

Today's leaders may even be drawing on some celebrated examples from history, such as the consolidation of General Motors by William Durant or the morphing of Wrigley's from a laundry soap to a chewing gum company. These leaders may be adopting a "world-view" or be putting on rose-coloured glasses by assuming that growth through mergers and acquisitions is not only a valid course of action, but a necessity.

Winston Churchill once remarked that men occasionally stumble over the truth "but most of them pick themselves up and hurry off as if nothing ever happened". This may help explain why businesses would engage in flawed mergers and acquisitions, year after year for more than three decades, without learning that there are pitfalls to be avoided. It may sound odd that such stark lessons are not learned by successive leaders, but world views, and biases are powerful agents.

There is ample evidence that organizations do not learn from the mistakes made by others. There had been several large oil spills in Prince William Sound, Alaska, before the Exxon

Valdez ran aground. A nuclear accident similar to the one at Three Mile Island had occurred some months before in the Tennessee Valley Authority. The product tampering that occurred virtually every week in North America did not seem to cause the makers of Tylenol, Aspirin, Ball Park frankfurters and other products to put effective safety measures in place. It is logical, therefore, to assume that the lessons of failed mergers and acquisitions are no easier to codify and pass on to senior managers in other corporations, or down through time, than are any other business lessons.

The role of "integration managers" in charge of mergers and acquisitions illustrates the unique personality types that may succeed in, or are at least drawn to, such deals. This type of manager may feel aloof from the organizational chart. The command and control chain is foreshortened. He is like a "cop" demanding results from all levels. One such manager says he feels as if he is "the CEO" of the deal. Others suggest that integration managers could be models for the manager of the future.

Often there's an emotional high in a foreshortened organizational chart, time line and decision-making loop. It could be that observers and the integration managers themselves are simply describing a fairly typical executive addiction to the adrenalin rush one gets from deal making and crisis management. This is a powerful addiction to control. The return to normal times through the rejection of a potential merger or acquisition would result in a crashing descent from this high. Even if some mergers and acquisitions constitute unproductive or busy work, they are irresistible to many leaders. Thus, the personality of the leader is a fruitful area for investigating the existence and nature of leadership failures.

In addition to emotion and ego that seem to play such a large role in big business deals, other research shows that quite different cognitive and decision-making powers may be needed to make mergers and acquisitions succeed. Decision-making has been found to fall into three categories:

- Skill-based (almost automatic, such as driving)

- Rule-based (following rules or procedures), or

- Knowledge-based (creative).

Mergers and acquisitions usually feature a rapidly evolving series of events where decision-making based on skills or rules would not normally succeed. If these types of decision-making skills are more-or-less evenly divided in an executive population, this would suggest that about two-thirds of all senior executives would be unsuited for such work. To generalize, the law, engineering, and accounting are based on facts, research, and rules. Yet senior management teams draw heavily on these professional areas when what seems to be needed are other skills. One researcher describes using inappropriate and unproductive techniques as "active inertia." In this case leaders and managers rely on their modes of thinking and working that brought success in the past. They simply accelerate the process of failure.

Traditional decision-making is a laborious process compared with what is needed to take quick advantage of a rapidly evolving business situation. Making decisions involves the identification of the problem, the generation and evaluation of options, and the choice and implementation of options, followed by more evaluation and the modification of more action.

This linear methodology will not work well in rapidly escalating situations such as emergencies and the fast-paced world of mergers and acquisitions.

The technique required in this different environment is described by the experts as "naturalistic" decision-making (NDM). Situations requiring NDM feature fluid and changing conditions, real-time reactions, ill-defined goals, ill-structured tasks and knowledgeable people. Mergers and acquisitions often feature elements of missing data, shifting and competing goals, real-time reactions, real-time feedback to changing conditions, high stakes, time stress, and other factors.

The technique used by those trained to respond to dangerous emergencies is called "recognition-primed decision-making". On-the-spot-decisions are driven by recognition of situations and patterns. Those decisions are re-evaluated constantly based on the latest information. In fact, emergency responders tell us they don't make decisions–they simply take appropriate action.

In the recognition-primed decision-making model, action is key. Experienced responders usually pick a workable option for their first attempt. Action is modified and improved by a constant assessment of the situation and further potential options. They don't try to decide which may be the best course, they just react to avoid known or observable dangers and re-evaluate their actions as they proceed. Mental simulations keep the decision-maker in a constant position to act, with the aim to satisfy, not optimize.

I must acknowledge that there are examples of successful mergers and acquisitions. Perhaps the most often cited is the record of achievement at GE Capital Corporation, a division of General Electric. GE Capital was originally formed to help and encourage consumers to buy appliances made by its parent company. During the 1990s, however, the CEO of General Electric used GE Capital's financial acumen and muscle to target companies for potential acquisition. From 1993 to 1998 it completed more than 100 acquisitions, resulting in a 33% increase in employees and a 100% increase in net income.

The CEO at General Electric at that time was Jack Welch. He was described as "feared and confrontational". He fired more than 100,000 employees in his first five years as CEO (1981-1986). Even when economic times were good, Welch encouraged his senior managers to replace ten per cent of their subordinates every year!

Mr. Welch himself quotes one executive as saying "Jack and I have been friends for eight years, and our wives see each other all the time. ...but he wouldn't hesitate to get rid of me." Another GE executive "checked himself into a mental hospital after an encounter with his CEO. Yet another, who struggled with obesity, was so worried that Welch would think him a fat slob that he had his lower bowel stapled—an operation that left him with chronic diarrhoea".

During his 20-year stewardship of GE, the company's value rose 4000%. When he retired from GE in 2001 he took a severance payment of $417 million, the largest such payment up to that point in history. In 2006, Mr. Welch's personal wealth was estimated at $720 million. However, in spite of all the accolades he received and wealth he accumulated for shareholders and himself, all was not entirely well at GE.

When he became CEO, General Electric had just made a billion and a half dollars in annual profit, with Reginald Jones at the helm. Mr. Jones was one of the most admired businessmen of *his* generation. However Jack Welch, who was personally selected by Mr. Jones to be his successor, promptly cut back on General Electric's Research & Development efforts to reduce expenses and increase profits. The result has been that a company that takes credit for first marketing the incandescent light bulb, the x-ray machine and unbreakable plastic, hasn't come up with many revolutionary products in years.

A chemical engineer by training, it turned out Mr. Welch's real strength was not R&D, but appealing to Wall Street with what has been called financial engineering. His wizardry is explained in this way by John Cassidy in The New Yorker:

> "Say that G.E. has a stock-market valuation of four hundred billion dollars and profits of ten billion dollars, which means that its stock is trading at forty times its earnings. ...Now assume that G.E. buys another company with a stock-market valuation of twenty billion dollars and annual profits ...of two billion dollars. What is the value of the combined company? You might think the answer should be four hundred and twenty billion, but that's not how Wall Street sees it. If investors continue to believe that G.E. is worth forty times its earnings, the new valuation will be four hundred and eighty billion dollars. As if by magic, sixty billion dollars will be created."

Mr. Welch's legacy as a wheeler dealer is secure. GE Capital was the real engine of profits for Jack Welch, accounting for almost half of the revenues of the parent company. It is really a bank—one of the world's largest. Indeed, it now calls itself a bank. When Mr. Welch took control of GE, it was an industrial powerhouse. Now it's something different.

In 1951, the CEO of General Electric commissioned a high-level task force to identify key corporate performance measures. In addition to profitability, the list included market share, productivity, employee attitudes and public responsibility. The report was silent on how these should be judged and it doesn't seem as if GE valued these other metrics as much as the immediate bottom line.

Times change, but even if corporate profits were the only manifestation of success, how do we explain that despite the dubious track record of acquisitions and mergers so many corporate leaders continue to pursue this very risky strategy? Corporate officers have access to the same information as academics and journalists. Their lawyers and accountants can investigate mergers and acquisitions in similar industries over time, or read of the celebrated failures that are frequently in the news. Why then would this trend of mergers and acquisitions continue for so long, despite evidence of its dubious benefits? What is it in today's business culture that allows, and perhaps encourages, many top executives to follow a path that they know (or should know) to be strewn with financial and personal land mines?

We know that senior people make decisions in different ways and these can affect business outcomes. Emotion, ego and even childhood trauma may be involved. In order to understand and explain the business and communication failings of modern managers and leaders, it may help to take a closer look at what constitutes leadership and the types of individuals who aspire to lead.

The Nature of Leadership and Management

How do we define the terms "leader" and "leadership? A dictionary tells us the former is "a person or thing that leads...a person who is well fitted to lead", while leadership is defined as "the state or position of being a leader...the qualities of a leader...the ability to lead".

That seems straightforward at first glance but let's look deeper at a business organization. It also uses the term "management", defined by the dictionary as "control, handling, direction". Yet a leader may also control, handle, and direct and a manager may be in a state or position of leading.

If we make a broad generalization, we can perhaps say that leaders are at the top of organizations and managers are one step lower in rank. The term "managing director" is used more in Britain than North America, but I know of at least one

Canadian company in which the President reported to the Managing Director. The terminology begins to obscure simple distinctions such as giving and taking orders–or position on the organizational chart.

If leaders are above managers, then it might also be true that managers are more often in the trenches, dealing with issues, people, assets, and systems, while leaders concern themselves with more motivational and conceptual matters. This might be consistent with some schools of thought which hold that management is the implementation of known systems, whereas leadership involves breaking new ground. Standards can address known systems, but breaking new ground is an adaptive challenge needing new approaches. Once those new approaches are mastered, they become standards to be implemented with management and supervision. So, even a good working definition changes over time, with the people involved and with the task at hand.

I still find these distinctions unsatisfying because we know that a leader may regularly perform management functions and vice versa. So let's broaden our search to look at leadership in history and in non-business settings.

As noted earlier it is not uncommon to hear the names of Winston Churchill, General George S. Patton or Charles de Gaulle in general discussions of leadership. These are just three well-known leaders from three different cultures, and others may come to mind, depending on context. Perhaps, ironically, it is also hard to imagine a detailed and analytical discussion about the leadership styles of these icons while they were in their prime. Perhaps it is the benefit of hindsight, but these leaders seemed to make decisions and act on them; their actions did not need validation by the word "leadership". Their leadership was self-evident. Yet today, corporate executives discuss their leadership styles at length and the business literature examines how various senior executives fit into leadership categories.

Given the violent history of the world, it is no surprise that the imagery associated with leadership often concerns the military. Both de Gaulle and Patton were generals and Churchill began his career in the cavalry. Even today military terminology such "lock and load", "take no prisoners", "in the trenches", "troops" and so on is heard regularly in the workplace.

It seems natural, then, to draw parallels between business management techniques and command and control practised by the military. The concept was borrowed from the military around the turn of the twentieth century and is still in vogue in many organizations. The irony is that my work with approximately 2,000 senior military officers as well as studies of the military literature show that this top-down decision-making concept has never been as universally useful as the doctrine implies.

THE MILITARY MODEL

The bayonet has been an instrument of war for hundreds of years of recorded history and was probably one for thousands of years before that. It may have had its beginnings as a sharp stone on the end of a stick. However, for the last three hundred years, the bayonet has been of limited use.

The plug bayonet, used around 1700, rendered a musket unusable, since the muzzle was literally plugged with the blunt end of the instrument. In the US Civil War, hospitals and field medics reported very few bayonet wounds. Yet fifty-five years later, the fixing of bayonets and marching toward enemy trenches was standard procedure in World War I. In that Great War, soldiers had difficulty wielding their long rifles within the narrow trenches. Elongating the weapons with bayonets may have actually lessened their utility. Yet decades after the bayonet had lost much of its utility, tens of thousands of men marched to their deaths, pointing them straight into machine gun fire. It is said that some machine gunners went mad at the slaughter.

Even more astounding, the bayonet was standard issue in World War II and can even be found on some modern rifles today. There was even a bayonet charge during the Falklands War. This illustrates the tenacity that many organizations display in clinging to useless or destructive policies, despite empirical evidence to stop.

Similarly, command and control was impossible and ineffective when World War I commanders, far behind trench lines, seemed unaware of the futility of infantry formations marching toward machine guns. Yet, these commanders repeatedly ordered troops to go "over the top", condemning tens of thousands to their deaths. Command and control was as outdated as the bayonet.

Certainly, if a soldier with an empty rifle were facing an enemy two feet away, the bayonet would have been useful. Similarly, if a boom were coming overhead on a ship and the watch officer shouted "duck", command and control would be very useful–even life-saving. But both the bayonet and command and control seem to require special circumstances to prove their worth.

In World War I, British troops not only subscribed to the command and control doctrine, but were also hampered by class-consciousness. There's at least one story of how a lost British officer near Vimy Ridge would not take directions from a private soldier. The officer took his troops into harm's way and probably died rather than break with tradition, rank and class.

Canadian troops took Vimy Ridge when French and British troops could not, in great part because of their egalitarian backgrounds, fostered in the rough-and-tumble Colony. Much of the work involved in trench warfare was exhausting manual labour. This was familiar to rural farm boys and woodsmen, but not to British troops, whose officers achieved their ranks largely as a result of class. The unorthodox Canadians once booed an officer off the parade ground for being late, destroyed a theatre because they did not appreciate the movie and generally showed limited decorum and deference. These were court-martial offences in other armies. But it was this individualism that made victory possible at Vimy.

Canadians developed the trench raid in which anywhere from dozens to thousands of soldiers tested German defences, captured enemies for interrogation, and killed or wounded thousands. Unorthodox Canadian officers recognized the importance of the machine gun. They used their own in an unorthodox manner for indirect fire, over ridges, as one would use artillery.

Fine calibration of artillery pieces made them more effective against the enemy, prevented many friendly-fire incidents and made creeping barrages more effective. Similarly, one officer with a scientific bent used the new field of acoustics to pinpoint enemy artillery and destroy it.

The most unorthodox tactic of all was the official flouting of the major tenets of command and control. First, massive rehearsals were held well behind the lines, using flags and markings on the ground to represent trenches and machine guns. Officers on horseback simulated creeping barrages. Most dramatically, every soldier was thoroughly briefed on routes and objectives and given a map. The idea of ordinary soldiers being entrusted with all this valuable information at that time was ground-breaking and unorthodox management. But egalitarianism worked. Vimy Ridge was taken. Command and control has its place, but the lesson of history is that its utility and value is not universal.

Another military lesson involves dealing with errors. Missteps abound in military history. Many can be blamed on the "fog of war", because when the action is in progress, it is difficult for everyone, including the commander, to know exactly what is going on. Much effort is expended to counter the fog of war, which commanders know will prevail during battle. Commanders know that a "hot wash-up", or debriefing and discussion, after the encounter will reveal errors and omissions. They not only expect these, but schedule formal "appreciations" before the event to gain all possible information, and follow up with debriefings to determine lessons learned.

I don't know if any business corporations subscribe to the military concept of the fog of war. I've never heard it mentioned during all the years I have worked with and coached senior executives. Perhaps they should remember that they will occasionally be in thick fog.

In the case of mergers and acquisitions the analogy might be that CEOs and others responsible for the venture are yelling "charge!" behind the lines, ignoring the significance of new technology, techniques, markets and shifting trends. They are clinging slavishly to missions and plans, even if reports back from the field are telling them they need to change tactics. CEOs need to take the longer view—as do good military commanders—that in all probability things will not go as planned. Circumstances and conditions can change and when they do, tactics need to be adjusted even if the overall strategy remains.

Leadership Requirements

My experience of working with business entities is that the term "leadership" is often used simply as a catch-all or metaphor for the fact that something has gone wrong:

"The leadership was lacking..."

"The problem was in the leadership..."

"There were leadership issues..."

"There's no leadership..."

In fact, "leadership problems" is a phrase that I've heard used to cover everything from sexual harassment, drug abuse, fraud, the padding of expense accounts, and general incompetence. It is as if modern leaders are supposed to be chaste, monogamous, honest and competent. Under these criteria it is relatively easy to know when leadership is lacking. Yet surely the term leadership implies something special, and not just the absence of improprieties.

The term leadership is also used as a spur to action with everyone from grade school children to young officers in the military, and from teenage athletes to rising executives:

"Show some leadership..."

"What we need is leadership..."

"With your leadership, we can really go places..."

But what exactly does this mean in behavioural terms?

To the World War I commanding officer, it might have meant pulling out his service revolver and shooting one of his own men who had broken rank to turn and run away. The officer's leadership may have saved many other lives by preventing a stampede. To the young soldier in Vietnam just fifty years later, it might have meant putting a fragmentation grenade under the bunk of the recent "90 day wonder"—the young ROTC officer who was so zealous he was likely to get some of his ranks killed. Sometimes the pin on the grenade was pulled and other times not—it depended on how much leadership was required for the circumstances. A grenade with the pin left in was just a warning. "Frag" became a threatening verb.

For some executives, leadership is keeping people employed in tough times. This is sometimes true for entire cultures. Working in Japan reveals a far different attitude toward job security than exists in Western countries. Returning to my hotel late at night I'd find three or four people behind the reception desk instead of the more usual one in North America or Europe.

These workers would be filling out forms by hand—work that a computer could easily do. The view there is that consumers should pay more to keep people in their jobs.

In North America, job security is seen as an unnecessary expense for shareholders. Not surprisingly senior executives feel under pressure to show leadership by cutting jobs, costs and assets in order to show more profit in the current quarter. When the quarter is done the more ambitious will look for even more creative ways to cut costs to bolster their reputation for "competence". As a result, these corporations may have created a generation of workers who assume that working life involves no stability, no loyalty and no pension. It is hard to look to workers for increased productivity and profits when their long-term outlook is so bleak.

Certainly leadership means more than profits. But what else does the term imply? If leadership only involves getting things done, then leadership becomes indistinguishable from productivity. If some leaders are born and others made and still others have leadership thrust upon them, then statistical averages would dictate that a corporation or political jurisdiction might do as well appointing or electing almost anyone at random to high office because that person would have as good a chance as anyone else to do well, especially with unforeseen challenges.

If leadership involves persuading others to perform as desired, jail guards, rapists, con-artists and some of history's notorious dictators could be classified as effective leaders. If it also involves getting people what they want, then some dictators would still qualify, having harnessed people's darker desires. If the definition is cross-referenced with what is good for people, then perhaps some authors of diet books are great leaders (until a contradictory diet theory appears). If it is cross-referenced with what is objectively good (health, longevity, peace, good-will), then many leaders, including Jesus Christ, might fail the test, considering that our world is still far from perfect.

Some leaders employ the practice of "rallying the troops"–mobilizing a team for a common purpose but this ignores at least three aspects of leadership.

First, it does not seem logical that a leader can always be exhibiting leadership. Sometimes both the leader and those being led need a rest from direction and activity. Leadership sometimes involves fostering and even exhibiting "follower-ship", or the ability to follow instructions from others. There are times a leader must act alone or cause others to act as lead-ers. The leader may have been the prime cause of another per-son's action, but in large corporations, governments and armies, subordinates are often too far removed from the leader to rely constantly on that leader's direction. Individual action must be taken, and that is a form of leadership.

Second, it is not always a team or a group that takes action or achieves a purpose. It may not even be a common purpose. Many leaders must challenge conventional wisdom and motiv-ate groups and teams to do things that others think will fail, or are considered the wrong course of action. So the leader may be motivating himself, individuals, groups or teams. S/he may also be motivating those categories of people to change categor-ies–to form into a group or a team or separate from the group or team, and act as an individual for a new purpose that has arisen. This recognizes both the episodic nature of leadership and the need for self-motivation and action by leaders.

Third, the purpose should be positive, however difficult

that is to define. Thus, a more specific and practical definition may be that leadership involves motivating oneself and others to achieve a clearly defined, positive purpose. The term "clearly defined" speaks to the need for leaders both to define objectives and use effective communication to impart these to colleagues.

Winston Churchill is revered as a great leader. He is credited with helping to save the world from Nazism and preserving democracy. Yet his non-war years were not so memorable, further pointing to the notion of time, chance, and context playing a role in the nature of leadership. He held high office for more than six decades, so longevity might be a criterion for leadership success. (This would exclude Bobby Kennedy, John Kennedy, Martin Luther King, Alexander the Great and others who died young). During Churchill's career, he switched political parties several times. So consistency is not necessarily a prerequisite for leadership. Just before World War II, he was seen as a lonely and pitiable figure having lunchtime drinks at his club. Members were warned to ignore the old man for fear he would bore them with his stories, theories and fears of war. So with regard to leadership qualifications, being right, just, and loved is not necessarily the key either.

Should morality be central to leadership? If so, then John Kennedy and Bill Clinton might not qualify. If respect for the rule of law were a criterion, perhaps American leaders who launched military campaigns for dubious or spurious reasons would not qualify. If it were bravery, then would Teddy Roosevelt who, despite being shot in the chest, gave his scheduled speech before receiving medical attention, qualify? If so, would US President William Henry Harrison, who had or caught a cold on his inaugural day and yet stayed out to give the longest inaugural speech to that date, caught pneumonia and died, also qualify? Is catching a cold less heroic than getting shot? Or is not attending to one's health and well-being just foolish, regardless of the circumstances?

Even past successes or failures may not be much of a guide to leadership qualities. General Earl Haig, the British military commander, could hardly be considered a success for yelling "charge!" well behind his own lines in World War I when his men were waist and even chest deep in mud at the front. Napoleon, one of the first leaders fully to understand public relations, lost horribly and left thousands of troops to die in Egypt, but went home to proclaim victory. George Washington, virtually a deity in modern America, lost the majority of the battles he fought in the revolutionary war. Lincoln lost several of his early elections, as did Canada's John Diefenbaker.

Many leaders have had little in their resumés to prepare them for the burdens of office. Lincoln had only very brief militia experience before becoming Commander-in-Chief, and Bill Clinton resisted the draft. Pierre Trudeau, from a wealthy family, had dabbled in travel, writing, and the academic life until almost fifty years of age and then dominated national politics. He had no military service. Ronald Reagan's preparation for ending the Cold War was as an actor in B-movies. So early productivity, prudence, or related experience may not be necessary criteria for displaying leadership.

Like intimacy, one knows leadership when it is there and misses it when it is gone. Like the amateur art patron, a follower may not know a lot about leadership, but knows what s/he likes. Like pornography, it's hard to define but easily spotted when viewed. In the end, one may be left with time, chance, and the review of history, not with objective criteria to define leadership.

We often think of leadership as involving charisma. Even if a leader obtains office through rational and legal means or is promoted because of competence, s/he often succeeds or fails as a result of personal qualities. The Chinese philosopher, Mencius, captured the power of charisma. He noted that when we are "subdued by force" we don't submit in our minds, "but only because ... strength is inadequate". But, "[w]hen men are subdued by power in personality they are pleased to their very heart's core and do really submit".

But what of the personal history and qualities that leaders have? Anecdotal and popular accounts indicate that leaders may be of above average height, Napoleon notwithstanding. They may have superior education, notwithstanding Bill Gates who dropped out of Harvard after one year. While we often think of leadership as a sophisticated, urban, and urbane phenomenon, it is remarkable how many leaders come from small towns. In my experience, the North American mid-western small towns and prairies provide a seemingly disproportionate number of leaders in the oil industry and military.

Self-sacrifice may also be a common leadership trait. Lyndon Johnson famously took heart pills while giving speeches and returned to smoking after his heart attack. Richard Nixon stood for long periods while campaigning with Anwar Sadat, despite doctor's orders to rest his leg while suffering from phlebitis. The sports hero who plays hurt, the soldier on the battlefield who achieves an objective despite severe wounds, and the modern high performance executive are all related. In order to understand and address business failings of modern managers and leaders, it may be useful to pursue the notion of self-sacrifice.

THE WOUNDED LEADER

Personal determination may be a valuable element of leadership. For far too many in the world of business, however, it has become the primary, and sometimes the only, element. Instead of being seen as a means to an end, displaying determination itself becomes the goal. This kind of leadership may be judged not by the goals achieved, but by suffering absorbed and endured.

Perhaps many of these CEOs could be described as wounded leaders. The hard-driving approach to business, the take-no-prisoners attitude to their colleagues and employees, the flamboyant personal life and questionable corporate financial legacy are not results produced by a healthy person. These may be characteristic of the kind of person who is conditioned by background, circumstances, and personality to pursue a destructive path to an ill-defined success.

Sigmund Freud postulated how men began to diminish themselves in order to accomplish their goals. Sexual energy diverts attention from other matters. Freud said that the first man to sublimate sexual desires excelled in other areas.

Even in literature the larger-than-life qualities exhibited by many leaders appeal to the majority of readers. The hero in Gothic novels is strong and healthy at the beginning of the story. He is spectacular, powerful, and in fact, he is too much so for the female protagonist. He is threatening, alluring, but unavailable to the female because he is married, betrothed to another, off at war, or on an adventure. Pain is experienced by these two characters as they circle each other, lives entwined, growing closer, then farther apart, then closer again. A resolution is needed. They are made for each other, but bizarre circumstances keep them apart. The pain only subsides when an equal or greater pain is inflicted on the hero. He suffers the psychological pain of losing his betrothed in some hideous accident or at the hands of a rival. Worst of all, the incident causing death may have been meant for him, but his betrothed stood in through mistaken identity or implausible circumstances. This psychological wounding diminishes the hero's power. Moreover, if the cause of the diminution also involved the death of the betrothed, the events make way for, and make necessary, the heroine. The hero is not only now accessible, but needs psychological nurturing by the heroine.

In another scenario, the hero is physically wounded. He loses capacity for a time, and may even suffer long-lasting effects such as paralysis, loss of sight, or loss of a limb. Either way, he cannot or does not want to resist the heroine. He needs her, or wants her, or is simply accessible through diminished capacity. They live happily ever after, with her as a caregiver. He accepts her as the best he can do in a bad situation. She obtains a prize otherwise unattainable. He may be damaged goods, but she has him. He is the wounded hero that most female readers would naturally be drawn to–perhaps more so because of his wounds.

More recently, the psychological literature has dealt almost as dramatically with wounds and trials of a different nature. Childhood hurts are carried forward into adulthood. The wounded adult adopts certain behaviours in compensation. Among these behaviours is the wounding of others.

THE WOUNDED
ORGANIZATION

S ome academic researchers have found it useful to conduct critiques of emotional and cultural aspects of organizations and policy making. This type of work supports the notion that a wounded leader may influence the personality of his organization and its behaviour. Wounded leaders may bring with them what has been described as a huge "well of fear" that fuels the abusive behaviour of adults. This may also fuel the behaviour of their corporations.

These researchers have drawn parallels between personality and corporate culture. Few harried husbands, fathers or wounded leaders would fail to identify with the "trick-cyclists, keeping upright and steady simply because they move forward so quickly". (Maguire, John, "The Tears Inside the Stone: Reflections on the Ecology of Fear", in Scott Lash, Bronislaw Szerszynski & Brian Wynne (eds), Risk, Environment & Modernity, London:

Sage Publications, 1996.) If a leader or corporation is not moving forward, fearful stagnation might result. Worse yet, a pause might result in self-examination and coming to terms with the wounds.

Fear generated by childhood abuse and self-doubt plays a larger, but unrecognized, role in the emergence and shaping of social, economic, cultural, and political structures. Fear may blind us to ways of making clear, life-enhancing decisions and being constructive. In addition, it may cause the passing on of hurts and fears to co-workers and even entire organizations. Conversely, a person who has been supported and whose nature has been confirmed will act constructively, not destructively. Nor, it seems evident, would this person build an organization that acts destructively.

Studies cite the dangers of getting "the testosterone flowing" to the detriment of the organization. Wounded leaders seem to treat corporate mergers and acquisitions as some sort of life-or-death military operation. Military and macho terminology are common. One company called its teams working on due diligence "Commando Squads". Team members were presented with 18-inch bowie knives engraved with their names, as well as the name of the target organization. While no doubt an extreme manifestation, this macho trophy would seem to suit many senior men in business.

THE WOUNDED CHILD

To understand the wounded leader we need to look back at the wounded child. A central concept in the wounded child framework is depression. Male depression is rarely diagnosed, first, because it seems unmanly and second, because we think of depression as a passive state. In males, depression manifests itself more in overt behaviour such as physical illness, alcohol and drug abuse, domestic violence, failures in intimacy and, the manifestation most relevant in this case, self-sabotage in careers.

Depression and its manifestations are traced to childhood. Several researchers recognize this linkage and have spelled out the consequence of adult abuse of children. Gender-specific rearing techniques cause young women to exhibit a withdrawn affect, whereas young men are encouraged to act out in childhood and thus do so, even when depressed as adults. Some research goes so far as to speculate on the actions of such brutal historic figures as Hitler, Stalin and the Romanian dictator

Ceausescu. They suggest that because of their own victimization as children they feel compelled to hurt and wound others.

A man's tendency to externalize or "extrude pain" can make him psychologically dangerous. Too often the wounded boy grows up to become a wounding man, inflicting upon those closest to him the very distress he refuses to acknowledge within himself. Perhaps some leaders pass on their wounds to others, and even wound entire organizations.

Wounds may actually be badges of honour for males in our society. The sports star who plays hurt is prized, while men who exhibit the "wimp disease" are ostracized. Could it be that the overweight, hard-drinking, hard-smoking executive, who has serial failed marriages, is engaged in the corporate equivalent of playing hurt?

When playing and working hurt, some men do not acknowledge distress. In fact, they prefer to place themselves at risk than to acknowledge distress, either physical or emotional. Could it also be that these same men would rather put their organizations at risk than discuss their fears with accountants, fellow executives, and lawyers, all of whom might be able to help waive the CEO away from the flawed activity such as a merger or acquisition, or steer him toward the more productive one?

Compounding the problem and the complexity of the question is the fact that many of the counsellors to whom the wounded leader might turn are themselves wounded. Unlike the traditional nurturing that females exhibit, when male students disclose depression to their roommates, studies show they can be met with social isolation and often with outright hostility. Leadership is lonely and wounded leaders may be lonely for good reason–they would suffer even more by disclosing their wounds.

One might wonder why a depressed and wounded person would not choose to stay in the shadows and lick his wounds in private. Why would a wounded boy or girl choose a high profile, public position in later life? The answer lies in the concept of "grandiosity". This is sometimes called the "narcissistic defence", or the use of grandiosity to "ward off shame". Consider this: a common defence against the painful experience of deflated value is inflated value. A common compensation for shame is "a flight into grandiosity".

So the shame of not being good enough as a child, of being deprived of unconditional love by parents, of not getting picked for the sports team, or experiencing abuse, can easily manifest itself as bombast, bullying and the passing on of such shame to others.

Wounded leaders can achieve grandiosity or a "high" from a variety of activities such as "the rush" of physical violence, the applause of an audience, or a sexual conquest. Wounded leaders can also turn to the business imperative of making "a killing" in the stock market.

A key point in understanding wounded leaders is that hurt, shame, and wounds are "passed on" to others. The first important notion is that all young men are wounded. It is part of the brutality of boys' socialization and passage into manhood. Another way of describing this is that the wounded man is carrying around his own wounded child, as if in a "Snugli" similar to those that parents use to carry an actual child. This may be both a source of pride, and a physical burden. The senior executive carries around his childhood hurts, his extra pounds, heart disease, failed marriage and other ailments. He apparently succeeds despite these burdens, which mistakenly makes the success appear to be an even greater accomplishment. These wounds may even be carried with a sense of pride, or at least a dramatization of how much pain he feels within himself. Then, the pain is passed on, in part, to normalize it. In other words, misery loves company!

It seems that the wounded child hypothesis has some role to play in understanding both personal and professional behaviour, including the failures of modern managers and leaders. In fact, it may also assist in addressing such failures. There is a prescription for healing within the theory. On the personal level, the adult must empathize with the wounded child within to move toward wellness. The reason that healing must begin in this way is that the wounded child demands far more than any person or institution can offer. If a child has been denied unconditional love, witnessed trauma, or been wounded in other ways, how would a wife, friend, co-worker or even corporation possibly show enough empathy to compensate? The wounded child within would need to be given back the childhood years lost during parents' separations, fights and so on. How could any adult hug a wounded child enough or say powerful enough words to compensate for childhood hurts? The successful empathizer would also have to turn back the clock and change events to prevent the trauma from happening. None of this is possible.

What could an organization do to compensate that wounded child within the current CEO? How could there be enough profits, perks or accomplishments to make amends, or prove his worth? This wounded child prism seems to explain the Roman toga parties, daily flower deliveries, shower curtains costing several thousand dollars and the like that news reports have revealed as part of some CEOs' lifestyles. A wounded boy deserves all this and more to compensate for the visceral hurt experienced as a child. But the prescription for healing is not actually more indulgence. It is empathy–the kind of empathy that the wounded child did not receive in childhood. But the only person who can effectively empathize with that wounded child is the adult who intimately knows the past hurts–that same child in adulthood, the adult who carries the wounded child around in a Snugli.

Because they lack empathy for themselves, wounded leaders lack empathy for others. Wounded people seek to wound others because whatever pain or trials they inflict on others pale in comparison to the pain and trials their own wounded boy suffered. It is only through empathy for self, and the healing of self, that one can have the fortitude and understanding to show empathy for others. The route to healing is through feeling. A man cannot recover and remain emotionally numb at the same time; he cannot be intimate with others before establishing intimate terms with himself.

THE NARCISSISTIC LEADER

The story of Narcissus may also help to illuminate the reasons for wounded leaders' behaviour. In Greek mythology handsome Narcissus is so vain he cruelly rejects the advances of any and all admirers. The avenging goddesses take note and decide that he too will come to feel the pain of rejection when he finally confronts the person he loves most. He sees his own face in a pool of water and is smitten. But as he leans forward to kiss this beauty, the image disappears. When he leans back and the water surface becomes calm again the image reappears–until he tries to kiss it again. He cannot eat or sleep, but can only remain transfixed by his own image. He remains by the pool and eventually dies.

Psychologically, narcissists are extraordinarily sensitive. Criticism hurts because they are so thin-skinned. The modern Narcissus may be in love with his bank accounts, good looks, power or just about anything other than who and what he really is.

Of course leaders may need to be proud and confident on many occasions. They may need to exhibit these and other traits to motivate others, even if their display is only an act. The danger comes when their swaggering is not an act but a conviction of their strength and their determination to use it no matter what the consequences are to those around them and to their organizations.

There are countless ways a wounded, narcissistic leader can push himself and his organization toward disaster. The high-need achiever can try to progress and grow at all costs. A result can be serious corporate governance issues of the kind that have dominated the business press for several years. Another result can be the wave of largely unproductive mergers and acquisitions that have been a feature of corporate activity for decades.

What of hyperbole and hubris? What of wishful thinking? One of the best examples of overstating a case may be Monsanto's stating that genetically-modified crops are "the single most successful introduction of technology in the history of agriculture, including the plough".

Male covert depression, according to the experts, seems to contribute to a range of personal and professional problems. Depression, they explain, dries "up a man's capacity to respond to his environment", in part because of his incapacity for self-knowledge and thus an incapacity to love others. Narcissus is numb. He is detached from real sensation. He does not even recognize his own face. Wounded leaders are numb to the pain they cause others and their organizations. They might not recognize their own actions if they read about them in the business press.

The Grandiose Leader

Researchers know that leaders have various styles and that individual leaders may employ different styles for different circumstances. One of the styles or traits they've identified concerns emotional intelligence. This includes self-awareness, self-regulation, motivation, empathy, and social skill. As valuable as these traits are, many male executives have difficulty not just in expressing, but even identifying their feelings. Naturally, if you cannot even identify your feelings, then those leadership tasks that rely upon self-awareness and the harnessing of one's feelings and those of others are unavailable to you. Furthermore, while empathy is considered to be one of the most important characteristics for emotionally healthy leaders we rarely hear people praised, let alone rewarded for their empathy. Empathy is a word not commonly found in the business lexicon.

The detachment of Narcissus and the modern corporate leader may appear to have an advantage. If one must make tough decisions that hurt people with downsizing or extra workloads, perhaps it is beneficial for the wounded leader to be detached. If entire communities are hurt by plant closures and re-locations, the wounded leader might become emotionally paralyzed if fully involved in the town's plight. However, when that detachment becomes pronounced, it may inure one to suffering and sever connection to those being hurt. Moreover, the wounded leader may also become detached from the effects of his decision-making in general.

Grandiosity can cause leaders to be removed from the important actions that they must take with people and organizations. This might explain why so few mergers and acquisitions produce new value. The activity was undertaken, but the executive as prime mover was detached from the details and consequences of his actions.

The Unempathetic Leader

Instead of displaying empathy, which requires them to understand the hurt of others, many leaders may try to dodge the issue and divert attention by moving house, wrecking marriages, taking to alcohol or other drugs or demanding bigger perks. Each change helps the mind ignore the pain–for a time. But while the smoke screens of activities mask the wounded child within, these wounded executives may actually be doing the corporate version of what wounded parents do to their families. They pass on the hurt and shame to all those they touch.

The corporations, government ministries, hospitals and charities that may be run by wounded executives, perhaps become organizations that, in turn, systemically wound employees and those they must deal with. Many such organizations can be hampered in their quest for progress, profits or innovation because of these wounds. Society needs progress, innovation and profits. Workers and their families want and need the economic activity to fuel health care, education, drug research and the arts. Employees want meaningful work to fund home and family activities. Most people want to live better, longer and safer lives, but rightly worry more about the system not working. However, the system comprises everyone. Everyone has a stake in it working. It could be argued that the system is wounded, and the first step in healing the wounds lies in healing the individual.

When this healing process begins, one of the first things to occur to a wounded leader, after acceptance of the diagnosis, is that business life and success will suffer if he is required to do things differently. Wounded leaders have an enormous capacity for work. They often have charming and compelling personalities. They fear that they will lose their edge or the other gifts that make them apparent successes.

Wounded leaders find it easy to buy and sell companies, to close and move facilities, and to lay off employees–decisions that inevitably make many people angry and sad. As hurtful as these actions can be, wounded leaders convince themselves of several things. First, they are performing at their optimum. This is what they do, and do best. They do not have to change because they are successful. Why change success?

Wounded leaders like to be hyper-active. Tranquil times are abnormal; chaos is the norm. One reason that narcissists thrive in chaotic times is, in part, that they have been trained to do so. A normal day at the office would be mundane in comparison to the excitement generated by a wounded leader passing on pain in order to normalize. Others may create chaos merely to keep the adrenalin flowing. With their chaotic childhood background, wounded leaders can turn leadership into a psychodrama in which a brilliant, lonely person must gain control of himself or herself as a precondition for controlling others.

Wounded leaders find intimacy difficult. They felt alone as children, and stay in that comfortable, known place as adults. If the wounded child had to make it alone, and the wounded adult has made it alone, then colleagues, employees, their families and communities can make it alone as well. Wounded leaders do not make good mentors, because intimacy is a prerequisite to good mentoring.

THE ERSATZ LEADER

There is another possible manifestation of the detachment found among leaders, which might help us understand and address the business and communication failings of modern managers and leaders. In a familiar office scenario we've all seen, an unproductive worker carries a file or piece of paper down the hall, stops in for coffee in colleagues' offices and double-and triple-checks mundane matters in lieu of productive work.

The unproductive activities of these office workers are often an open secret. One might call their activity *ersatz* work. The work has the aura and trappings of productivity, but does not add value to the organization. The ersatz worker begins the day arranging phone messages and files on his desk. Then s/he gets a coffee and a doughnut from the stand in the basement. On the way to and from these early morning errands, s/he stops at the Xerox machine to make a few copies of an interesting clipping for co-workers. Checking social media prolongs this process. It can be mid-morning before the ersatz worker has to confront actual work.

In fact s/he may be working in an ersatz department. This department produces reports, study documents, clipping files and background memos to circulate. Ersatz departments hire advertising agencies, research companies and consulting firms. Focus groups, questionnaires, brochures and reports are a result. It could even be argued that the term "meeting" has the connotation of ersatz work about it.

Leaders are not immune from engaging in this type of activity. Modern executives may have time on their hands because of labour-saving production techniques and economic cycles. At the same time, leaders feel that they must do something. So they may fill up the time with busy work. Is it possible that some busy work could even be large-scale mergers and acquisitions?

The notion that executives have time on their hands may seem odd in these fast-paced days of electronic communication. But it could be these same labour saving devices–computers with sophisticated software, smart-phones etc.–allow executives to have time on their hands, especially as they become more senior. Today, 50-year-old workers aren't anywhere near as tired as were their forebears 100, or even 50 years, ago. More likely, they are just bored, as management guru Peter Drucker wrote. Some retire early, change careers, do volunteer work or take up hobbies. But many stay on the job, well past the time when previous generations would be worn out both mentally and physically.

If executives do stay on the job, it stands to reason that the job is easier to do. There are some rewards for getting older in the knowledge economy. Office jobs get easier, unlike physical labour. Many managers and professionals can perform their job functions in less time with greater efficiency. Even Law Society billing regulations in many jurisdictions recognize this by allowing for a fee structure that takes into account not just hours expended on a project, but also benefit to the client, as well as years of service by the lawyer.

What do modern executives do with this extra time? Do they engage in busy or superfluous work? Does this help us to understand and address the failings of modern leaders and managers? For even casual observers who have worked in corporations, the notion of ersatz work seems plausible. It explains an observable reality of organizational life: the unproductive executive pacing the halls with a superfluous file. It should not be surprising that even the most senior people engage in busy work. Moreover, it is a short step for wounded leaders from busy work to bullying and bombastic behaviour. Both fill the void of time. It is an equally short step to assume that some corporate activity, such as mergers and acquisitions, occurs for its own sake or to fill the time of a senior executive.

In this environment, wounded leaders may turn to ersatz activities. I have accompanied them on lengthy trips ostensibly to motivate employees by holding "retreats" in the mountains or at the seaside; hold "blue sky" meetings and even negotiate mergers and acquisitions. These executives have all the appearance of being busy, strong leaders. Their activities are of the kind one would expect from leaders.

However, they may just be filling the void of time until more useful activities can be scheduled. In the meantime, there is an ersatz labour theory of value. In this version of Marx's theory, it is the activity of the leader that imbues the corporation with value. Wounded leaders fail to see the flaw in this theory. If labour by itself were the major determinant of value, a worker could pound a hammer into the ground in the backyard and become rich. Value is also created by demand, need, price, utility and other factors. Similarly, the mere fact that a senior executive is very busy does not mean s/he is adding value to the organization.

Ersatz activity often manifests itself early in a new leader's tenure. Many take up their new positions with vigour and vitality. I've worked with numerous "new brooms", who have high energy and vision. They walk the halls, stop off in subordinates' offices for brief chats and are generally engaged in management by walking around. After a few weeks or months, their approach changes. The hallway management dwindles. The office door closes. Formal meetings are more frequent and longer. Busy work or "activity traps" become a way of escaping the unmanageable tasks. This is the time in a new leaders' tenure when travel becomes attractive. Fact-finding missions to regional offices, ceremonial openings of new plants and mountain retreats may be a way to avoid facing the issues at hand–the geographic cure. Some researchers characterize the superfluous or busy work as "Flavour of the Month" managing. In this type of leadership, both senior executive and organization are particularly vulnerable to the latest panacea being touted by the newest addition to the business guru circuit.

Ersatz activity can be found in both personal and professional life. Psychologists have coined the term "Dad Zone" to describe the remote father puttering in the garage, tinkering in the basement, or installing insulation in the attic. Family members might want real interaction, but the father is absent from his own life through this ersatz activity. The organizational parallel is the "executive zone" wherein executives are found on unnecessary business trips, making lengthy bullet point presentations, commissioning irrelevant studies, and so on.

LEADERSHIP &
COMMUNICATION

There's no shortage of studies of the links between leadership and communication. There's clear evidence that good communication generates profits through increased productivity and customer satisfaction. Seen through this prism, communication is not a cost of doing business but an investment.

I know that effective communication can mitigate crises, reduce liability and save money. And we only have to follow the news to know that poor communication can aggravate and inflame crises. Poor communication takes the wind out of the sails of followers and can cause them to question the abilities of leaders.

It's been said that slogans, metaphors, and symbols are the "soft" version of leadership, management and communication. They are certainly popular in today's corporate culture.

However as the Western world's business dominance is threatened by new emerging markets perhaps our corporate leaders need to try something new to explain their vision and motivation. As it happens, one of the most frequently overlooked tools for effective communication and management is also one of the most powerful–the use of figurative language and symbols.

Over the years I have come to understand why symbols help leaders to achieve clarity. First, the repeated use of catch phrases, jargon, and buzz words has a tendency to dull their meaning. Many leaders may like to impress, especially when they get into new fields, by using the jargon of that field. Not only can jargon be confusing, but even the clearest of words can have ambiguous meanings. For example, many organizations in both the private and public sectors use the term "transparency". They hope it convinces people they are open and honest but they seldom define which of their activities they are talking about. If the word is not defined, transparency might mean that everyone can see and know about the unethical and improper things going on in an organization. Politicians nearly always promise to make government more transparent, but once they obtain power they stress the need for Cabinet confidentiality or security to protect "national interests"–selective transparency.

Effective communication requires a full, not a partial, understanding. Speakers need a full understanding of the topic, and the audience needs a full understanding of what was just said. This sounds simple, but this challenge has kept me in business for more than 25 years. Getting the whole picture requires us to "see" all the parts and connections. Some organizations are aware of this and have adapted their methods accordingly.

The company 3M uses what it calls "Strategic Stories"

rather than bullet points in their business planning. This technique causes the sales force to "paint" stories through word pictures. Stories and word pictures resonate more effectively than sterile words. In fact, it has been argued that bullet point business plans fail to reflect much in the way of thought or commitment. Bullet points allow people to avoid thinking seriously about how they can communicate effectively. Traditional printed decks or overhead presentations are no better because they are so generic. They offer a series of things to do that could apply to any business.

The 3M executives who use strategic stories believe that bullet points actually conceal inconsistencies in a planning or other communication document, whereas a full narrative will reveal any flaws in the logic because they are all too apparent. You can't tell much of a story with holes and gaps in it. Using such a technique, both communicator and audience can see where they are going and what needs to be done. Since visualization is so important, the logical next step of actually creating a visual representation of the matter being discussed is vital. Employees need both a clear "line of sight" and a visual representation in order to follow a leader or a strategy. All too often, however, annual reports, speeches, and corporate strategies are peppered with generic, vague terms like "customer satisfaction" and "environmental awareness".

There is an additional need for clear communication in the age of high technology and information overload. Communication is an area in which a person or an organization can achieve a competitive advantage. Attitudes, values, goals and the like can be considered as intangible assets that can help achieve that advantage. Here again, visual aids such as storyboards and icon mapping are the best tools to describe such intangibles. Drawing them causes them to become tangible and understood by both speaker and listener. It is through this understanding and the subsequent actions of buying, loyalty, referrals and so on, that these intangibles become quantifiable financial assets.

Time is money, and both are being wasted through poor communication. Weak policy statements with no "action commitment", and abstract reports, are common and will neither be understood nor acted upon by workers. Most meetings are characterized by ineffective verbal interactions and little follow up.

Many executives like to quote mission statements and vision statements. But, most of these statements turn out to be a muddled mix of values, goals, purposes, philosophies, beliefs, aspirations, norms, strategies, practices, and descriptions. They are usually confusing and boring. Not surprisingly, the muttered response from listeners is "Maybe–but who cares?" In fact many of the things said in these presentations are not even true. Few executives bother to probe beyond the superficial platitude to see if there is an underlying truth or body of supporting evidence for the catch phrase. This may be harmless in a training or motivational session. But even during real times of crisis, I have noted that senior officials are often guilty of wishful thinking and even outright lying.

Concrete, behavioural objectives, clearly stated, are needed to help achieve concrete goals. The information required certainly exists–somewhere–but unfortunately the complexity of modern corporations often makes it hard for executives to find it when they need it.

Much of the information about an organization is accumulated over a long period of time, without any plan or strategy guiding its management. The result is that much of the information is out of date, some of it is inaccurate, no longer relevant or misleading. Regular reviews of this material, updating and re-writing it is a good way of increasing the value of this important organizational asset. However, even if an organization has managed to maintain an up-to-date informational archive there's no guarantee its executives will make use of it (see James Robertson).

THE UNCOMMUNICATIVE LEADER

During many years of coaching leaders I have learned the vast majority have great difficulty describing their roles or explaining their ideas, beliefs, and goals. The coaching sessions always begin with introductions. One of the first instructions is "Tell me what you do". Most leaders recite their titles, which reveal little of what they actually do. When asked for clarification, it's not unusual for them to say something like: "I'm the team leader...which means that I lead the team". It becomes evident that many senior executives are at a distance from their own jobs. Phrases such as "I'm supposed to..." "I guess what I do is..." and the like betray dissociation, or at least a lack of connection with the job and job description.

The second toughest question asked is "What do you mean?"–particularly when it is posed to an executive who has just said that he wants to offer customers "an enhanced value proposition". When asked to clarify what that means, the same executive elaborates by showing a determination to "upgrade customer profit touch points". At about the fourth iteration, it becomes clear that there is no clarity for this executive or this company on this issue. The words seem to exist for their own sake, just floating in air.

Why does this happen? Why do individuals and organizations lack clarity? Perhaps many senior executives are overwhelmed by the complexity of the issues that they face and the organizations that they run. In individual sessions, leaders often reveal that they do not know what is on their corporate website. Sometimes they contradict company documents and in some group sessions it is not unusual for them to contradict each other.

Many senior people appear determined to achieve control, connection, and meaning. They are not sure what they need, but they know that something is lacking. For example, the head of a very successful financial management company was not responding well to questioning or to exercises designed to harness his skills, knowledge, and imagination. No technique would elicit information on what he wanted himself and his company to represent. He was not fully present in, or committed to, the exercise. As he psychologically moved in and out of the room, he did manage to recite a few positive words, such as "integrity...expertise...service" and so on. But then he got a better idea. He turned to his public affairs person and asked for "the list". She produced a document from a consulting company that had a list of positive attributes arranged graphically on a sheet of paper.

"There it is!" the CEO exclaimed in triumph. He had paid good money for such a list and seemed pleased to be able to use it in lieu of inventing one in the session. However, a glance at his list revealed that not one single word on it matched the half dozen words he had been reluctantly able to volunteer. Why did he think he could buy his corporate values, ethics, and goals on the street like so many cups of take-out coffee? Was it logical to outsource such a personal and important matter?

The experience with this executive is not unusual. I find most are psychologically distant from their messages, their colleagues, organization and the training sessions in which they are observed. Here are some more examples of uncommunicative leaders in my coaching sessions who didn't want to change:

- The Vice-President of a multi-national firm kept insisting he didn't know what was expected of him even halfway through the session. He was being asked to describe his job function. A future session was cancelled and the full fee paid, perhaps rather than pursue the hard work of coming prepared.

- In a pharmaceutical company, a senior physician attended for coaching on a major presentation in the national capital on the subject of intellectual property rights. It quickly became evident that he was unaware of the "Harvard Mouse" case, soon to be heard by the Canadian Supreme Court. The landmark legal case involved Harvard University's patenting a laboratory mouse.

- Ironically, in another session with a Canadian government official who was responsible for intellectual property matters, the only message put forth on the Harvard Mouse case was "it is before Ministers". Inasmuch as virtually all contemporaneous matters of public policy are put in front of the Cabinet, this was a hollow and tautological message. There could have been a discussion about the need for, benefit of, scientific implication of, or conflicting aspects of the case, without pre-judging Cabinet or Court decisions.

- A small group of pharmaceutical company spokespeople learned for the first time that its drugs were being sold over the Internet. They expressed surprise, but my researcher quickly found 300 sites on which one of the best-known prescription drugs in the world could be purchased.

- A telecommunications company executive was unable to state his employers' position on the regulation of a piece of new and exciting technology. In frustration, I asked to see the company's submission to the regulatory authority, and noted that a succinct position was contained on the second page of the executive summary. The document was, in part, authored by the spokesperson who showed little knowledge of its content.

A related challenge involves leaders and organizations that claim to have policies in place, but do not. I can't begin to explain why this happens–but here are some examples:

- An institution involved in a sexual assault case assured me that detailed policies were in place to prevent such occurrences. Policies forbidding two people to be alone behind closed doors without a witness, rules about socializing after business hours and such are common in many organizations, especially among social workers and educators. When I asked to review these policies, I found that they did not exist. In fact, one official handbook had a policy at odds with written policy in another.

- A residential facility caring for developmentally-challenged people was facing an inquest into the death of one of its charges. I asked if trauma counselling had been offered to the care-giver who had been looking after the deceased. Senior managers said that such counselling had been offered, but was refused by the care-giver. The care-giver was in the same session and said that he had requested counselling and it had been denied. This misunderstanding had existed for eighteen months.

- An international nuclear association commissioned a conference at which I was a speaker. A delegate presented a template for a typical crisis plan that members should follow. It contained dozens of job descriptions. The author indicated that reading, let alone following, lengthy job descriptions would be counterproductive during a crisis. The delegate agreed that during actual crises the job descriptions are ignored.

- A medical device company experienced a supply chain problem and at least one patient, needing delivery of the product, died. Many others were inconvenienced or had adverse health reactions. We called the company's toll-free hot-line, but the phone rang repeatedly without being answered. When answered, it was by a person on a cell phone in an underground garage who rushed the call because the cell reception was intermittent. He lacked knowledge of the device and the disease and merely said "don't get it".

- A law enforcement agency installed a toll-free hot-line. The purpose was to receive information about money laundering related to terrorism and organized crime, as well as to provide information to callers regarding how they could comply with the law and spot suspicious transactions. One senior spokesperson mentioned the hot-line in a coaching session. I called the number immediately and was told by the operator that she could not provide any such information and that she could only pass my name on to the spokesperson who was sitting in the room with me.

- In the early days of the tainted-blood scandal in Canada, which also touched many other countries, I asked the appropriate authorities (clients) how blood collection and storage facilities were inspected. They could not provide a complete answer. I wanted to know if and when samples were taken, whether they were inspected visually, how often inspectors made rounds, and so on. The lack of complete answers was suspicious. It subsequently came to light in court cases and media reports that proper inspections had not taken place, resulting in the transmission of AIDS and hepatitis C to many transfusion recipients.

- One month prior to 9/11, I conducted training and simulations with an aviation concern in Washington, DC. The questions involved what the organization would do if someone rented a plane to crash it into The White House. We were assured this would not happen. When we pressed, the organization said the scenario was impossible because such renters of planes would both kill themselves and lose their deposits. We assured the aviation company that many people around the world would make that sacrifice. Moreover, at least one attempted hijacking in the past was for the purpose of crashing into the White House and a small plane once crashed on the lawn.

- Perhaps the most chilling incident involved spokespeople for a nuclear facility that was being questioned about the theft of overalls and other materials contaminated with radiation. The concern was that the thieves were going to make a "dirty bomb". One nuclear official protested, stating that "pants cannot explode". We had to explain that a dirty bomb was made by blowing up contaminated materials to spread radiation.

Because of the frequency of these surprising challenges I began giving participants additional guidance about what to expect and what was going to be required of them. Regrettably many still don't read the material before attending an expensive strategy or rehearsal session.

Improving
Communication

In the Hollywood movie *Cool Hand Luke* a prison guard beats a prisoner almost to death. In surveying the situation, and as a commentary on his inability to get the prisoner to do exactly as ordered, the guard states "What we have here is a failure to communicate".

A popular notice in office cubicles advises, "The beatings will continue until morale improves".

There is most often a grain of truth in humour and popular culture. Whether one communicates through memos, e-mails, bullet points or the lash, there seems to be a consensus that failure to communicate is prevalent and is at the root of many interpersonal and organizational problems. Moreover, it seems to be understood that more effective communication may be at the root of better human relations, more profits and more efficiency.

There is evidence of this in both personal and organizational life:

"We weren't communicating", can be reason for divorce.

"He just doesn't have the communication skills", is one reason for denying promotion.

"The Great Communicator" summed up Ronald Reagan's skills.

"We need to communicate with our customers better" is a euphemism for the need for higher sales.

These and other common phrases indicate that effective communication is vital to successful leadership and the creation of value in the modern organization. We know that information can be power. Information may also be money in the bank in an information-based economy. In addition to the anecdotal evidence of the value of communication, academics and researchers refer to "knowledge capital". There is even a new category of labour called "knowledge worker" in this information age. But for knowledge to become a valuable commodity, it must be imparted through excellent communication skills. In fact there may be few skills more necessary for the modern leader than clear, effective communication.

SOCKO®

The good news is that good communicators are not born. They learn to communicate. Speeches and presentations should not feature long, complicated sentences filled with parenthetical phrases and jargon. Use simple, short phrases, no longer than a few words. This is a way to create the speed and stimulus-response action of speech.

SOCKO® is an acronym for *Strategic Overriding Communications and Knowledge Objective*. Each word presents an opportunity to discuss the characteristics of message making, speech, the needs of listeners, and other relevant topics. The fact that SOCKO® sounds like a word that might be used to indicate impact in a cartoon panel is not accidental. So, even if you forget what each letter stands for you know you need to construct a message with impact.

You can find a more detailed explanation of SOCKO®s and how to develop and use them in my book "Speaking, Writing and Presenting in SOCKO®s", but here is a brief description.

Strategic

There should be the same level of strategic thinking in advance of oral communication as there is before sending a written document. People read, re-write, edit and polish the written word. Out-loud rehearsal, in front of an audience, videotape and play back is the verbal equivalent. Many executives resist these exercises because a videotape of their performance is much more personal and less forgiving than a written memo. The memo can be subject to debate, whereas a grimacing face, inaudible voice, and negative body language are unmistakable on video.

Overriding

Making a speech or presentation involves having to decide which bits of information you should use and in which order they should be arranged. Getting started can be the biggest challenge, but there is an easy solution. Imagine all the assembled data of your topic contained in an iceberg. The tip of the iceberg–the top 15 percent–is reserved for what you think is the most important message. The remaining, supporting information stays below the imagined water line until the most important message is used, at which point another message floats to the top–and so on.

Communications

This is to illustrate the difference between oral and written communication. Leaders should be thinking about using a different language, which is visual, simpler and very different from written language.

It does not have capital letters, commas, bullet points, bold letters, or other graphic elements to help make a point. A writer does not have intonation, pauses, body language, facial expressions, gestures, pacing, or tone to make a point. Both writers and speakers have their own versions of these elements, but must work in different ways to communicate effectively.

One of the most important tools for good oral communication is repetition. Repetitive letters and memos seem unpolished. Editing is supposed to remove the same or similar phrases from documents. But speech must have repetition for clarity. Speech should also feature shorter sentences and more visual imagery.

Knowledge

Facts, data, and statistics are important. Employees, customers and others will not understand why the manager or executive does not have such knowledge readily at hand. But there must be care taken in how this knowledge is communicated. Depending on the circumstances, audiences may lack the technical or background knowledge with which to understand facts, data, and statistics. Research shows that some words trump other words. Some statistics will trump other statistics. But the vast majority of pictures and images trump both words and statistics. Choose wisely.

Objective

Many business leaders set measurable, behavioural, quantifiable objectives for themselves and their colleagues. They also set such objectives for oral communication in presentations to staff, in meetings, and so on. Business leaders have grappled for decades with management by objectives (MBOs), management by results (MBRs) and a variety of other metrics. For oral communication, the metrics should be as specific as an audience applauding, an employee group working harder or smarter, a business colleague signing a contract, a client ordering a product, or a judge dismissing an action. Even mundane presentations and meetings should feature smiling, nodding, writing, and concrete follow-up action. The more concrete the objective, the more concrete will be the language and result.

AIDS TO COMMUNICATION

In today's fast-paced business world, technology is used, databases are accessed, material collated and so on, in order to cause the movement of information from one person to another to be more complete, efficient and effective. But if one only discusses technology such as e-mail, voice mail, PowerPoint presentations, social media and newsletters, it is possible to lose sight of the personal nature of inter-personal communication. Indeed it has been pointed out that communication may work better without technology. For example, rumour is a very effective means of communication. Rumour moves quickly and efficiently through an organization. Most MIS or Knowledge Management heads would be pleased to enjoy the success of the rumour mill!

And PowerPoint doesn't help. A headline in the *New York Times Magazine*, "PowerPoint Makes You Dumb", would be humorous if it were not dealing with the Columbia Accident Investigation Board at NASA and its report on the crash of the space shuttle and loss of the crew. The Board indicated that NASA relied too much on PowerPoint slides which were "so crammed with nested bullet points and irregular short forms that it was nearly impossible to untangle". NASA's presentations were dealing with a life-threatening situation–but managers failed to spot it.

The article's general criticism of PowerPoint is that it forces people to mutilate data beyond comprehension, pressures presenters to use less information, and allows a speaker to dodge his responsibility to make his message coherent. It concludes as follows:

> Perhaps PowerPoint is uniquely suited to our modern age of obfuscation—where manipulating facts is as important as presenting them clearly. If you have nothing to say, maybe you need just the right tool to help you not say it.

To be fair, the blame may not lie with PowerPoint itself and its developers and programmers. At heart it is just something that projects slides. A "slide show" can be a very entertaining and informative process. Too many organizations, however, have chosen it as their medium of written communication.

To some extent this is understandable. Most executives spend their days working with written reports, memos, e-mails, performance appraisals, spreadsheets, and other such documents in print or on a computer screen. So it's not surprising that when they have to address a group of colleagues or employees they rely on truncated versions of their written reports–bullet points on slides.

The printed word may appear to be safer and more familiar.

A leader who is concerned about looking foolish, being caught in a wrong answer, or is worried about having to connect on a personal level with co-workers and subordinates may feel much safer with the printed form of communication. Computer screens, printed reports, e-mails, and planning documents do not feature the unpredictable give-and-take of a bull session with staff or even a frank boardroom debate. We need something different to get our messages across.

Speaking Visually

A picture is worth a thousand words–except in most boardrooms, business speeches and presentations. Executives trying to communicate goals, strategy, and plans continue to use inefficient words when they should be embracing the transition to a new visual and *digital* language.

The first step on the road to a new visual language is the notion that the written and oral languages are significantly different. It may be immediately apparent that they are some-what different, with the written language having more formal constructions. But there are other differences. There are usually more technical terms in writing than in speech (contracts, specifications for landscaping and building, etc.). There are also more rigid rules of grammar (not only...but also, neither... nor, either...or). These occur in print regularly, but in oral communication, one often speaks in a manner that bypasses these formalities.

A further difference involves the linear nature of print. Writers use "the latter" when referring back to a list, and refer to "said" document. Both constructions may require the recipient to re-read the foregoing to determine what is being referenced. There is punctuation in print but not in speech–in spite of comedian Victor Borge's hilarious routine in which he gave crazy sound effects to punctuation marks and then told a story with appropriate noises sprinkled throughout. There are gestures, facial expressions, tone, pausing, and other elements that help communication in speech, but punctuation, capitalization, paragraphing, and the other graphic elements of print are not available to a speaker.

Non-verbal elements, or "paralinguistics", act as visual punctuation. However, despite the common purpose of communication, body language, paralinguistics, and imagery may constitute three separate languages. Since imagery can be transmitted either verbally or through non-verbal gestures and body language, it could be argued that there are just two languages. Regardless, the elements in the separate, but overlapping, languages constitute a significant difference between print and speech. A Venn diagram (named after the mathematician) might show a fifty per cent overlap, and thus a fifty per cent difference between written and oral communication.

The second step towards a new visual language is to recognize that speech is the senior of the two languages. Speech came first. Most cultures have an oral, story-telling tradition. The written language is only a way of codifying what was said. However, because of the permanency of print, paper, and books, and the apparent ephemeral nature of speech, many people tend to mistakenly revere print at the expense of speech. This causes many executives to try to imitate memos, specifications, and contracts when speaking. Perhaps they feel that this will sound more impressive, or that it is more business-like. But they are using the wrong language. Imitating the written form creates formality, distance, and denseness, all of which are incompatible with the capabilities of the voice (pausing, pacing, etc.), or the needs of the ear.

This formal print construction is also incompatible with the personal and emotional needs of co-workers and subordinates to feel connected to the boss and the project.

The ear does not ingest information or translate it well. It has the greatest difficulty with long print constructions, featuring subordinate clauses, parenthetical remarks and lists. So the speaker must choose another tool: the spoken language. The spoken language is characterized by simplicity, clarity and brevity. It is visual and symbolic. Moreover, the spoken language is bolstered by the speaker as a platform for visual aids conveyed by the body, voice, and face.

Storyboards

It is dysfunctional enough when executives cannot quickly describe the attributes of one of their company products, commonly found under kitchen sinks or in medicine cabinets. The challenge can be much greater when the topic is technical and it is vital that the message gets through. The answer is a system which has helped many technically knowledgeable professionals. These include scientists, nuclear regulatory officials, lawyers, and diplomats who reach the point in technical discussions where more words will not clarify.

What I ask them to do is imagine making a Hollywood movie on the topic they have to address. This means they first must develop a storyboard. Moving cameras and crews around is so expensive that movie makers construct a graphic treatment of the story first, so all involved know exactly where they are in the story and what comes next. For business presentations, speakers need to communicate messages that conjure mental images to match the tasks with which their uses are associated. As in Hollywood movies, this efficiency, economy, and clarity is best achieved through the use of storyboards.

This technique also addresses a problem that might be termed the sender-receiver dynamic. The speaker has an image in his or her mind. That image is translated into words, many of which are metaphoric, metonymic, symbolic, referential, or ambiguous. These images are translated into words, spoken by the sender, and then received by the listener. The receiver translates these words into images in the mind. This can be a clumsy system that leaves ample room for misunderstanding. But after working with many thousands of leaders I can say categorically that using word images reduces ambiguity. The vast majority of senior executives make a significant breakthrough using the storyboard technique. Some find it difficult, and a very few say they don't like it. But to a person, they have a clearer message at the end of their training session than they had at the beginning.

Digital Versus Analog

Another way of thinking about word pictures is to compare the old way of recording sound and pictures–analog–to the modern way–digital. Words can be considered *analog* and word pictures *digital*. Words are only analogues for what the speaker wishes to convey, and thus may be interpreted by the listener in a different way from the one intended. Word pictures are truer to the original thought in the speaker's mind and thus may suffer less distortion and interpretation in the listener's mind.

An example from audio or video recording will illustrate. Analog recording (remember old home VCR or audio cassette recorders?) involves storing electronic impulses on magnetic tape. Some time later, those impulses can be read or lifted from the tape by a magnetic head and sent down a wire to make a diaphragm vibrate. The end result sounds very much like the original sound, but there is degeneration over time, over distance and with duplication. Digital recording is a different process. Sound is transferred into binary codes to be retrieved at a later date. There is a debate among audiophiles, but there is no proven or significant degeneration over time, or distance, or with duplication.

The US Supreme Court has deliberated on whether one can burn the real, digital, American flag. They probably would not entertain a case involving burning the letters "U. S. F-L-A-G" written on a piece of paper. The paper image only constitutes an analog version of the flag. There is the actual flag, and there is also the analog representation of a flag (the letters on a piece of paper).

The two are different, and viewers and the courts react differently to them. (Just to complicate matters, the real, digital, actual flag is probably also analogous to, symbolic of, metonymy for and referential to country, duty, war, sacrifice, freedom and other matters. This simply illustrates the layers and levels of communication possible and available).

The artist Jasper Johns was exploring this more than forty years before the Supreme Court was. His representation of the instantly recognizable American flag, coloured with a waxy material on newsprint makes the viewer concentrate on whether s/he is reacting to an actual flag, the idea of a flag, the materials, or the artistic technique. One also wonders whether Johns is mocking or praising art, the flag, the artistic process, the viewer, himself or something else. It should not be surprising that an artist would be able to offer a succinct illustration of levels and layers of communication.

A similar example involves the fact that one cannot sit on a piece of paper with the word CHAIR written on it. The word and the paper are only analogous to a chair, not an actual chair. The communication is incomplete if one only uses the word chair. If a regional VP is opening up a new divisional office, and calls a furniture store to order a chair, there could be any number of things waiting there when s/he arrives: an Obusform, Bentwood, a rocker, a stool, swivel and so on. To obtain the desired chair, s/he needs digital communication. S/he needs a word picture. If s/he says, "Please get me one of those high, leather, wing-back, over-stuffed, diamond-tufted, library chairs of the kind you might see Winston Churchill sit in, puffing on a cigar", s/he is more likely to get what s/he wants. S/he might have to discuss colour, price and legs, but the digital communication has eliminated most of the chair styles that might be considered.

The point of this examination of digital versus analog is that most official communication from leaders in industry and government is analogue. I've seen this every week in coaching sessions for 25 years. The message means something in the mind of the speaker, but it does not translate into the minds of the recipients very well. The message has a long way to go, from image in the sender's mind, to Roman letters (if print), into speech, across the air to the eyes and ears of the recipient, and finally translated into an image in the recipient's mind. It is hard to imagine that the final image, let alone the action or attitude resulting from that image, is very close to the first image in the communicator's mind. But using digital word pictures makes the image in the mind of the sender translate more effectively into the mind of the receiver. Moreover, a digital image of a chair is closer to the chair pictured in the mind of the speaker. Any analogue of that chair, especially words, lessens the meaning because the recipient has so much leeway to interpret just what kind of chair is under discussion.

Impediments Between Senders and Receivers

The mind works at several times the speed of the eye, the ear, or the mouth. This is why the mind wanders when one is listening to a speaker. This is why speakers use visual aids to try to present more information to engage more of the mind. Some explain this wandering of the mind with the phrase "spare thinking time". They contend that the best listeners use this spare time wisely to reinforce and engage in the messages received. But a good communicator wants the audience to be fully engaged with the topic. S/he does not want the listener to have the option of thinking about distracting matters. Analog words leave room for interpretation. If the mind is seeking meaning from the first sentence in a presentation, it is not properly focused on the second sentence. Digital word pictures, followed by other compatible and supportive word pictures, keep the mind engaged, and powerfully reinforce each successive message.

Communication is not synonymous with semantics. Words are communication tools, but it is the meaning that they evoke that is more important. Language, and thus communication, is based on meaning, not grammar. People listen for and react to meaning, not words, grammar, idiom and semantics. Obscure words, poor grammar, unknown idioms, and improper semantics can mask meaning, but meaning is the important aspect of the exchange. The two-year-old child who says "Me love Mummy" is not admonished for failing to use the subjective case. Similarly, the two-year-old child who uses an expletive is not complimented on her vocabulary. Parents listen to the meaning, according to scholar Daniel N. Robinson.

Not only are non-verbal and other visual elements more important in oral communication than one might immediately think, but these elements are vital to the thinking process too. Some thinking may be language-based, but it is not as powerful or prevalent as image-based thinking is. A person may recite words in the mind's ear to scan for meaning or information. This is a similar phenomenon to having a popular tune playing in the mind. But while that mundane function is going on, the brain is engaged in another level of thinking. The tools on this level are not words, but images, word pictures, colours and shapes. These two types of thinking are going on at the same time. Images, including incongruous ones, pop into the brain, while speaking or listening. The effective speaker who must inform and motivate wants any thinking or picturing in the recipients' brains to be consistent with what the speaker is saying. Words alone will not cause this congruity, but word pictures are more likely to achieve that end.

The importance of images and non-verbal signals is illustrated in the non-verbal icons used in signage. They evoke meaning, not words. Take, for example, a sign with a red circle and a diagonal red slash through it. We know instantly what it means. If there is an automobile in the middle, we don't think of the words "No cars allowed". If there is a cigarette in the middle, we don't think of the words "No Smoking". We get the message far more quickly than if we had to read the words. We may also mentally construct the words, but there's no need–that's just excess brain capacity at work. The proper behaviours are already in motion (not doing something), and the use of excess brain capacity is superfluous.

Asian pictographic languages illustrate this point. Much, but not all, of Japanese and Chinese written language consists of ideograms that have evolved over centuries. There has also been some reform lately, as when the Japanese Diet or Parliament debated whether the pen stroke that symbolises a broom should be removed from the ideogram signifying "woman". In Chinese pictograms, there has also been an evolution from a literal attempt to represent something concrete to a more metaphorical one, where the pictogram or ideogram is not instantly recognizable as the object described. This is similar to the journey that the Roman letter-based languages have taken toward the metaphorical and symbolic. In pictographic or ideographic language, there is not as pressing a need to translate from words on a page to a word picture in the mind. The transference can be instant, particularly when the pictogram is literal and has not evolved to the metaphorical.

Here are Chinese pictograms for "sun".

Each of the five mean "sun", but the pictograms on the left are the oldest and are successively newer in turn. The newest is on the extreme right. The reference to the sun seems obvious in the first three circles. When the pictogram becomes a square, the representation is more metaphorical, thus needing translation.

Here are the Chinese pictograms for "rice field".

These, too, range from the old to the new, from left to right. The earliest pictograms may have alluded to the shape of a field, or a farmer demarcating his land. They may also have referenced the rice seed with its root or planting techniques. The newest pictogram may evoke the rigid lines of plantings or more formal demarcation lines of fields.

Next are Chinese pictograms for water.

The first three contain obvious references to water and the last is more metaphorical. The last image may evoke a river or stream, and its tributaries, when viewed from high above.

Another example of the instant transference from pictogram involves the purchase of coffee. There are very palatable cans of hot coffee for sale in vending machines on Tokyo streets and in office buildings. Different buttons produce different blends with varying amounts of sugar and milk. After several trips to Japan, I found it interesting to see how quickly Westerners adapt and reach the point where they can decipher the symbols for the various types of coffee on the vending machine, and instantly understand which one they want. They can read the ideograms expressing sweetness, whiteness and strength more quickly than they can read the English translation.

Take a look at the Japanese pictogram for coffee:

珈
琲

You'd think it would take some time before a Westerner could recognize this complex a symbol, since it does not visual-ly represent coffee, liquid, bitterness, heat, or any of the other characteristics of coffee.

But that's not the case at all–Westerners catch on quickly.

Not only are images immediate and effective communica-tion vehicles, but words themselves may actually have only a patina of meaning that quickly erodes. Children know this from the game of repeating a word so often that it becomes gibber-ish. They say "chair, chair, chair, chair, chair...". Not only is no chair imagined at the end of this exercise, but gales of laughter are usually the end product. The word "chair" evokes its meaning mainly in context. In the home, a chair may evoke style. At a train station it may evoke rest. In the office it may represent prestige. The child's game is entertaining because the word "chair" loses its meaning and becomes just an interesting sound. Similarly, the corporate annual report and executive presentation may lose some meaning, because the mission, vision and value statements are pro forma and hollowed out from overuse.

The Filter, the Medium, and the Matrix

As discussed, the regional Vice President who is ordering a chair can do so more efficiently by causing an image of that chair to appear in the mind of the person being asked to order the chair. But there are many impediments to making this happen. These impediments can be put into three categories: the *filter*, the *medium* and the *matrix*.

The *filter* involves all of the elements that scrape meaning away from that image in the sender's mind, as it journeys to the receiver's mind. First, in written communication, the image must be translated into Roman letters. In speech, a decision has instantly been made as to what few descriptive words to use and which of the dozens that could have been used to leave out. With speech, there is intonation, body language, facial expressions, pausing, pacing, breath control, and so on. Some of these elements may add meaning rather than filter it out, but the net result is a further communication difficulty. The receiver ingests this visual and verbal information through the eyes and ears. Research shows that the eyes and ears filter out most of what they encounter. Humans can detect only a relatively large movement in the field of vision, compared with animals that must look for food on the forest floor. Humans cannot see in much of the light spectrum. Because of the placement of the eyes in the front of the head, humans have limited peripheral vision compared to horses and other animals. The ears filter out much of the decibel range that many other animals hear. Whatever the receiver does receive must then be translated back into an image in the brain. That first image in the sender's brain has come a long way, and each translation has scraped some meaning from the image. In addition, the process may have added superfluous or distracting elements to the message during communication. These elements might be called communication barnacles. At the same time, the non-verbal techniques of the sender, whether intended or not, have modified the message.

Once a portion of the sent image is in the receiver's brain, more distortion occurs. The brain is not a neutral medium having no effect on the messages it receives. In the brain are stored images and experiences. The brain has had the benefit of education and experiences. It has well-worn synaptic pathways. The resources in the brain are far more voluminous than the content of a few sentences said by a speaker. Messages may evoke positive or negative stored images, build on agile mental reflexes, or get lost in ambiguity.

This ambiguity is pervasive. The image of a chair may evoke countless types of chairs. This can be called the *group* of images or experiences evoked by communication. This large group of evoked images is one reason why messages fail to get through to recipients, or, if transmitted effectively, fail to motivate in the manner in which they were intended. If the messages motivate, they may do so in diverse ways, depending upon the experiences of the recipient. Leaders delude themselves by thinking that their messages are received clearly and consistently by diverse groups of people.

In addition to a large group of images from which to choose, there is also a grid of stored experiences. When a concept such as "chair" is introduced, the brain scans a grid or matrix containing all of the stored experience it has had with chairs. Such experiences may include the time a chair broke, the marks left in the floor after leaning back on the rear two legs of a kitchen chair, sitting on Santa's lap, and so on. It seems axiomatic that the myriad experiences one may have had with chairs will colour the meaning taken from a message about chairs.

In summary, only portions of messages are received and retained because of the above impediments. The message is filtered so that only a part of the original message reaches the recipient. Non-verbal clues from the sender either support, divert, or detract. Moreover, the grid and group scanning that occurs in the brain distracts and detracts from the message.

It thus seems that the communication task is threefold. Speakers should strive for less filtering in order to have more of the intended message reach the listener. Body language should be supportive of the message, not distracting; the brain should either evoke the image intended, or limit the number of distorting images elicited. Finally, the scanning of the group, matrix, or grid of distracting and irrelevant meanings and experiences should be at a minimum. Word pictures go a long way to accomplishing these tasks.

Visual Aids

We know that that visual aids can make presentations more memorable by increasing retention by up to fifty per cent. But presenters still must wrestle with what type of visual aids to use. Much of what is used as visual aids in traditional presentations is alpha-numeric. For the most part, words and numbers are not actually visual aids. Perhaps the letter 'A' and the symbol #1 evoke excellence, winning, or leadership. The symbol $ evokes money, prosperity, and perhaps security. It might also evoke debt. Some numbers have cultural or religious meaning. However, for the most part, numbers, letters, and words are not visual aids. In fact, they may have the opposite result of the intended one, as in the case of the multiple meanings that the dollar symbol can evoke.

Even clear visual aids, whether icons or alpha-numeric can be a distraction in typical presentations. While a speaker is transmitting words and non-verbal elements of communication, a screen is also transmitting bullet points, percentages, occasional icons, and headings. When the speaker is on the first item, the audience has usually read down to the third. When the speaker arrives at the third, the audience is finished. When the speaker is near the end of the list, the audience is back at the beginning for a review. One is never synchronized with the audience. The typical leader's road-show presentation, while putatively achieving the goal of transmitting information to staff at plants and regional offices, is not usually transmitting much of substance or many clear messages about which managers and workers can take concrete action.

Undifferentiated Thoughts

One key to clarity in communication is for speakers to achieve the goal of differentiating their ideas from myriad others that could be evoked by their speech. This is the communication equivalent of a unique selling point in advertising. Speakers need to be careful about what thoughts they evoke in the listeners' minds because there are few, if any, undifferentiated thoughts. Thoughts are specific, even though words may be vague. Word pictures evoke more specific thoughts and images than words, and are thus the appropriate tools to use when the goal is to differentiate ideas and messages.

To illustrate, I sometimes ask clients to imagine a bird. I tell them it isn't large like an albatross, nor small like a hummingbird. It is not any particular colour; not light or dark and it makes no particular sound. Its feathers are neither sleek like a penguin's nor long and traditional like an eagle's. Not surprisingly, they find it impossible to imagine an undifferentiated bird. The word bird can certainly evoke an image but different people will quite likely think of different birds. When John Lennon sang "Free as a Bird", few listeners imagined a penguin, vulture or chicken. That phrase, imprinted on our psyche, evokes mobility, speed, and grace. Naturally, there are limits to the specificity that one can expect to transmit. An eagle is free, as is a seagull, hummingbird, and many other species. But the ability of a hummingbird to hover, the strength of the eagle and the ubiquity and banality of the seagull help dictate whether these are appropriate images for a particular communication purpose.

The speaker cannot delegate the responsibility of picturing specific images to the audience. The speaker must take responsibility for ensuring that those images which support a message are evoked.

LEADERSHIP AND THE LIMITS TO GROWTH

Traditional economic theory suggests that there are few limits to growth. There may be differing opinions as to whether to use monetary, fiscal or labour market changes to foster growth, but many economists seem to feel that growth can always be achieved. This is sometimes described as the uncritical ideology of economic growth, rather like an unquestioned faith in "the market".

Until recently, growth seemed assured. North America is an excellent example of apparently limitless opportunities. For generations, relatively unskilled workers could use a shovel, a gun, axe or a trap line to achieve riches. Western expansion and new technology prolonged this phenomenon after population growth and environmental degradation in the East. In an expanding economy, many entrepreneurs could seemingly do no wrong. An expanding economy, increased immigration, the migration to cities, inflation, and the baby boom papered over many mistakes. Low margins on stock in warehouses rose as inflation caused consumers to expect higher prices each year. It looked like the bubble would never burst, and even if that bubble burst, a new one–high-tech, bio-tech, micro-tech, nano-tech, and dot-com–would take its place.

During this time of expanding economies in the twentieth century, there were great physical strides made: bridges, sky-scrapers, cars, aircraft and space exploration. Researchers have dealt with this type of mind-boggling change in detail, but not so much with the human capacity to deal with change. The type of change that is well documented is technological. There is a consensus that such change happens enormously quickly. Mass-media attention and higher education levels have contributed to a change in what is considered to be proper business conduct. This has also put business activities under tremendous, and far more informed, public scrutiny.

Remember, there are different types of change. Some change is useful, some is just change for change's sake. I describe the latter type as redundant or residual change. Redundant change happens because there is so much momentum for change that it cannot be stopped. Changes in fashion, some consumer goods such as automobiles, furniture, and home renovations (especially bathrooms and kitchens) might fall into this category.

Residual change is a version of redundant change but happens more as a by-product of necessary change. Automakers added FM radios to cars as a necessity because of the increased use of the FM band and the deterioration of the AM band. Then they added cassette players, then digital technology, and compact disc players. This change just might be called necessary.

But along with it came other innovations that were made simply because they were possible. Digital car radios now have search functions that can scan the frequencies for the next receivable station, and can be programmed to find favourite stations. Some car radios are designed to function as speakers for cell phones, and others can provide facts about the song being played.

Many consumers, however, never learn how to operate the new technology that results from this residual change. Even those who do understand how the new technology works often physically cannot master it because miniaturization has reduced the size of the buttons so much that a consumer pushes three buttons at once, when just one should be pushed. Cell phones will perform dozens of functions, many of which consumers do not or cannot use. In the handling of cell phones, buttons are sometimes pushed randomly, and the phone then performs unintended functions. This is a result of residual change arising out of the necessary invention and improvement of cell phone technology.

Many may share a frustration with change. It is even the subject of comedians' jokes—but there also can be a deadly side to it. Airline pilots crash planes because they do not know what their instruments are telling them. Workers in the control rooms at nuclear and chemical plants cannot distinguish important from unimportant alarms. Many modern crises are a result of these types of interactions between people and the technology they use. Researchers have named these phenomena "socio-technical accidents".

There are limits to how small you can make a keyboard, cell phone or car radio and still make it function practically. Practical function involves the technology interacting with human

beings for the purpose intended. These limits extend throughout the economy. Video recorders that permanently flash 12:00,
programmable dishwashers that are not programmed, and
underused home computer capacity are merely metaphors for
the redundant and residual change found in the plant control
rooms, on the factory floors and in the executive offices of Western economies.

Certainly necessary change still occurs. Factories need
re-tooling, office furniture replacing, people need training, and
computers upgrading. In the case of computers though, redundant change is reflected in the wireless keyboards and flat
screens, the extra power purchased, and the e-mail for everyone
regardless of need. It is not unusual to hear senior executives
complain that they are being swamped with copies of mundane
and routine e-mails from juniors trying to prove how busy they
are. It may seem heretical to ask in the information age, but do
all employees need the power and capabilities that they have
on their desks and in their hand-held devices? Perhaps these
technological developments help employees feel as if they are
putting their stamp on their workstation and job function.

Similarly, even if unjustified, it is very common to find new
senior executives acting to put their stamp on their region, division, or company. Thus, reorganizations are undertaken, con-
sultants are hired, and new markets are sought in new ways.
However, seldom do those new profits sought through mergers
and acquisitions materialize, and about seventy per cent of all
consulting studies go unheeded by the commissioning corporation. This leadership activity sounds like a very expensive version of the executive carrying the file down the hall to look
busy. This is ersatz work from ersatz leaders.

Leaders may like change for several reasons. Change puts their stamp on the organization, and change and uncertainty are most familiar to them. Change is comfortable. If leaders operate well in chaos, others can and perhaps should work in chaos too, because, to the executive, that is what is normal. And it appears to be progress.

However, leaders need to be able to distinguish between the different kinds of progress. There is also a big difference between knowing about something and controlling it. The great progress made in the twentieth century in understanding the human condition, group dynamics and brain functions does not mean that these matters are being controlled. There are limits to the ability to do something about, or to change things, even as we learn more and more. The Hawthorne effect is a good example. Studies proved that a change in environment (lighting, colour, coffee break times) yielded an increase in productivity, even when that change was a negative (lower light, fewer breaks, etc).

Yet the practical application of this has limitations.

For example, there are physical limitations to keyboarding speed, regardless of environment. A very good typist in the 1960s may have been able to work at 60 or even 70 words a minute. Today's computers and their sophisticated word processing software may be able to help experts exceed 100 words per minute, however that's not very different from what was recorded in the late nineteenth century when the typewriter was invented. In fact, the typewriter was modified to the scrambled QWERTY keyboard in order to slow typists down so they would not jam the keys of their new machines. Perhaps programming computers to know the standard paragraphs preferred by executives might add even greater speed in the twenty-first century, and direct neurological connection to the brain might add even more. But I assume that proofreading will still take the same period of time, as will the reading done by the recipient. Moreover, I can't imagine an executive being able to dictate or write two documents at once–even if we changed the environment hourly to try to harness the Hawthorne effect.

The modern Olympic athlete wins a race as a result of being one one-hundredth of a second faster than the next Olympic athlete. This difference is imperceptible to the human eye yet can be worth hundreds of thousands of dollars in endorsements, book deals, and advertising contracts to the winner. So while Olympic records will be broken at the next games and perhaps at many in the future, the real, measurable progress is only marginal.

There are similar limits to physical prowess in the workplace. The person in the stock room can lift only so many boxes or pounds at a time. The person answering the phone can only handle so many lines and the executive has to sleep. The adult who is 5' 4" tall is never going to be taller than her co-worker who is 6' tall. Those workers can be assisted by ergonomics, robotics and ladders. But they have limits.

With all the evidence about the limits to growth, why do so many executives continue to foster the notion that all people and organizations have to progress at all times? Perhaps it is emasculating to aspire only to the status quo. The HR department might seem to be lax if its goal is to motivate a percentage of the workforce only a percentage of the time. The individual might be dismissed as ineffectual or not a team player if his goal is merely to maintain the status quo. Yet many workers only want predictability in their working lives–a regular shift, coffee breaks, lunch hours, weekends off and holidays. They derive their pleasure at home with their friends and families. Employers sometimes talk about the work-life balance, but in reality they still expect employees to want to progress and increase productivity on the job.

Farming provides a non-corporate analogy to help illustrate the limits to growth. An hour's drive from many North American cities there still exist small farms. My family owned a succession of such farms in three Canadian provinces for more than forty years. It was obvious that early settlers could live on one hundred acres in the fertile Eastern part of the continent. They cleared eighty or so acres, most for growing hay and some for pasturing animals. There would be a stream to provide drinking water for the animals, and a thirty-foot well dug for household water. Many of these wells still provide potable water today. A garden provided vegetables. There might be chickens, pigs and cows. This ended up being a small, diversified economy.

In a well-planned farm, something was maturing out of the garden between mid-August and the late apples that come after the frost in October. The gestation periods of cows, pigs and chickens, and their other contributions of milk, eggs, and meat are also varied enough that something nourishing was being produced each month. When it came time to sell any of these, the diversification proved helpful. If pork prices were down, pigs could be kept and a calf sold, or vice versa. Everything was a cash crop and everything was also either money in the bank or became preserves for the winter–a version of money in the bank.

Automation, fertilizer for the fields and drugs for the animals changed the premise of farming. These were designed to increase growth, perhaps indefinitely. Fertilizing the fields would vastly increase the yield of hay. More hay in the barn would support more cows.

But an examination of the consequences of these aids to growth reveals that many are mixed blessings. Large quantities of fertilizer on the field do help grow more hay, but that hay may break a mowing machine or bailer at harvest time. The barn might not be big enough to store the hay. Apple trees, left alone, are said to produce one third for the birds and worms, one third to rot on the ground and one third for the farmer. Spray and trimming increases the yield. But after a few years of chemical use, nothing will grow under the apple trees, and fences have to be built to keep livestock away from the toxic ground. Redesigning the barn to house only pigs might seem to be a good idea when pork prices are up, but not so good when disease devastates the livestock or when prices drop. Accepting the limits to growth and the safety in diversification appears to be logical when analyzed.

There was also an ebb and flow to work on the farm. Depending on the climate, crops and animals, planting and harvest times involved long hours. The term "harvest moon" refers to the need to be out in the fields after dark, with the farmer's workspace only illuminated by the light of the moon. Calving time, or farrowing time for pigs meant staying up through the night to ensure the health of both the mother and newborn animal. However, there are also cyclical down-times to traditional farming. Winter is time for wood chopping, machinery repair, sugaring (harvesting maple syrup) and such. But winter does not feature the frenetic activity of planting or harvesting time. Few farmers would seek out unnecessary busy work in these off times, as is done in modern corporations.

Systems theory allows the farm to be used as a metaphor for the modern business corporation. Researchers in this area have found that it does not matter whether a particular system is biological, social or mechanical in origin, it displays much the same properties as if it were the same basic kind of system. Interestingly, the father of systems theory was a biologist–Ludwig von Bertalanffy. Since unlimited biological growth is not possible, why would it be considered that unlimited economic growth is possible? This parallel, or this transference of lessons from one system or one part of a system to another, has been termed isomorphic learning by Brian Toft in the UK.

Downsizing, streamlining, specialization, optimization and miniaturization may seem like good ideas because they can be done and they are the trend. These and other management techniques may impress Wall Street analysts and shareholders. But inherent in many of them is a danger. Downsizing may make a corporation lack the critical mass of people necessary to act quickly and take advantage of opportunities. It may destroy the corporate memory. Concentrating on one product may be as dangerous in the factory as on the farm. Making a product more quickly may sacrifice quality control. Impressing Wall Street analysts may create short-term gain, but little of lasting value.

There are limits to growth–both personal and organizational. These limits, perhaps coupled with leaders' failure to recognize them, could help us understand and even address the failings of modern managers and leaders. The enterprise and the individual may not be able to grow, regardless of technique.

A Changing of the (Old) Guard

Change is a constant. Everything in our lives is in a state of flux. We grow, we age, change jobs, move house and alter our political views. Some change is good, some bad, some big and some small. Change is a word that business executives use all the time. Sometimes they mean big changes, such as closing or moving a plant and displacing hundreds of jobs. Sometimes the change is small–a change in the company logo. But possibly the smallest change witnessed in the last half century has been in the leadership ranks of the world's biggest business entities.

Take a look at the leaders of Fortune 500 companies, the biggest companies in the world ranked by gross annual revenue in US dollars. In spite of all the changes in the global economy–the collapse of Communism, the huge growth in Asian economies, the growing importance of South America and the large numbers of women joining the upper ranks of business–the vast majority of CEOs are White males from North America and Europe.

In 2010, companies based in developing countries accounted for 17% of those found in the Fortune 500. Three years later that figure had climbed to 26%. On that basis, analysts are predicting that emerging markets will account for 45% of Fortune 500 companies by 2025.

Steve Tappin, an American consultant, who works closely with Chinese and Asian companies, describes the current crop of Western CEOs as professional managers who incrementally optimize their companies for short-term gain. He predicts they're about to be leapfrogged by a new breed of CEOs running on an emerging market fuel, powered by dreams, entrepreneurship, innovation and belief. He says incrementalism is the cancer that will kill many Western companies.

Sallie Krawcheck, a former head of Merrill Lynch and Smith Barney, also warns that Western, predominantly male-run companies, are going to have to adapt and change to survive. They should understand that the inherent differences among genders and cultures are not things to be fixed, but are instead sources of strength. She suggests they change their evaluation systems to eliminate "cascading bias," in which the qualities of the existing (typically white, male) leadership team are reinforced and other types of skills are undervalued.

Perhaps it's not surprising that Western companies have, in recent years, focused on small gains rather than anything revolutionary. After all, the last "giant leap for mankind" was taken in 1969 when Neil Armstrong stepped onto the Moon. Septuagenarians who watched that momentous event could also remember the first powered flight, development of the automobile, the first radio broadcast, the advent of television, invention of the jet engine, nuclear power, the first humans to orbit the earth and the first heart transplant.

Those born after 1968 have had to be satisfied with the evolution of computer technology. Our digital world may be a thing of wonder but it has evolved only gradually from clunky boxes and wires to slim smart phones and tablets. It's hard to get too excited about a product that lets you watch a movie or live sports event on a tiny screen, or that lets you pay your bills while driving your car.

It could be that all inventions in the future will be evolutionary rather than revolutionary. If so, we may need to look at a new style of business leadership that prefers to take the longer view—one that recognizes short term fixes and profits may just be a short-cut to a dead-end.

Because of Western domination of the global economy over the last two centuries, leadership roles in corporate entities invariably have been filled by people of similar cultures and levels of education, who share the same goals and have similar thought processes. But now that the global marketplace is changing—and fast—where can we hope to find a new breed of leaders who will be able to recognize new opportunities and handle new challenges?

If future growth in the global market is going to come from countries in Asia, Latin America and Africa, perhaps we can look to them for guidance. Instead of insisting the world should do business our way, we may find ourselves forced to do business their way. And if we want to have any influence over how much we have to change, we better start studying other models and definitions of leaders.

Earlier, I used the example of pictograms found in some Asian languages to suggest how we could deliver more visual—and therefore more efficient—speeches and presentations. I've also found there's an Asian institution which may help us address our leadership and communication problems. The Karate Dojo features a hierarchy, mobilization of a team for a common positive purpose, and regular verbal direction. Yet few, if any, of the communication and leadership problems I've encountered in modern businesses, are evident in the Dojo.

It may be productive then, to examine the nature of leadership and communication in that setting.

It is customary to submit a grading essay when challenging for Black Belt. This contains a resume, academic achievement, fitness history, philosophy of Karate and other matters as assigned by Sensei. The essay package must contain at least one picture of the candidate in a Karate pose appropriate to his or her rank. Because of my age and rank I had earned the privilege of approaching some aspects of Karate with an unconventional creativity. In my 3rd Dan grading I melded my studies of business and the Martial Arts. I wouldn't normally be in my Dojo in a business suit, nor read my computer while standing on my head. But the combination of Karate, business and a physical challenge seemed appropriate. At my grading my Sensei's Sensei asked me to stand on my head in front of 200 or so Karate practitioners and their guests. He then questioned me to keep me in that pose for a time.

LEADERSHIP &
COMMUNICATION
IN THE DOJO

I originally took up Karate as a diversion from work. It didn't take very long, however, to appreciate there were serious lessons to be learned about leadership, communication, teamwork, and productivity, the very topics in which I coach my clients. In fact there are important lessons in the Dojo, for both student and teacher.

Dojo simply means training centre. Its leader is called a Sensei, which translated from Japanese means "one who has gone before". The issues the Dojo helps to illuminate include the mobilization of a diverse group, skills development, authority, teamwork, the episodic nature of leadership, and the temporary assumption of a leadership position.

With regard to skills, "Black Belt" merely means "master of the basics". It normally takes three years or fifteen-hundred hours of training before taking the test to qualify for a 1ˢᵗ Dan (degree) Black Belt. Two years later, candidates may test again, and, three years after that, the third degree can be attempted. My Sensei is a 5ᵗʰ Dan Black Belt.

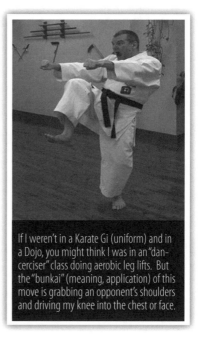

If I weren't in a Karate Gi (uniform) and in a Dojo, you might think I was in an "dancerciser" class doing aerobic leg lifts. But the "bunkai" (meaning, application) of this move is grabbing an opponent's shoulders and driving my knee into the chest or face.

A trainee in Karate is also developing the qualifications to teach the Martial Arts properly. Part of the tradition is helping and encouraging others, which suggests that teaching is an aspect of leadership, motivation, and organizational change.

In today's business world, leaders must deal with diverse employees, women and men of different cultures, races, language groups and ages. Dojo members are even more diverse. They usually have nothing in common except for the training in which they engage. There are several linguistic groups represented in my Dojo, and educational levels range from high school to post-graduate. Students appear to be from wide socioeconomic levels, with occupations ranging from bicycle-courier, student, the unemployed, to a few professionals in architecture, psychiatry, and so on. There is a visual artist, autoworker, solar power expert, military officer, and massage therapist. A typical class contains approximately thirty students who are much more diverse than those found in most places of work.

Employees in a workplace may all have experienced similar

training for their particular occupation. They may have similar educational backgrounds, as in medical or legal organizations. Ages may be similar, as a result of years required for promotions (partnerships in accounting or law) or occupations that only attract young people (shift work, IT, etc.). There may be professional standing and a governing body involved. There may simply be a shared experience in an office or institutional setting, which serves as a common denominator for an otherwise diverse group of receptionists, secretaries, managers and shop-floor workers. People who spend forty hours per week with each other develop more shared experiences, common outlooks, and vocabularies than those who spend three to fifteen hours per week together in a Dojo.

In corporate situations, a leader can call upon the professionalism or shared organizational experience to mobilize group members. This shared experience may involve common terminology and jargon. However, when people join a Dojo they do not have any common experiences.

In many fields, leaders can resort to a system of rewards and punishments to motivate their employees, students, acolytes or athletes. While a Dojo Sensei may have charisma, skills, and the ability to appeal to self-interest, s/he cannot reward or punish in any meaningful way.

Earlier, I referred to the storyboard used in the movie industry as a useful aid for improving verbal communications. Now consider for a moment the hierarchy of a film set. Theoretically the person in charge is the director–but it is the movie stars who are more powerful, more essential to the success of the project, and more highly paid than the director. Just imagine how chaotic a modern office or factory floor would be if some workers were being paid far more than the boss. Because he has little leverage with rewards or punishments a film director has to have a different set of managerial skills–one that relies on the self-sufficiency of the workers. It is the professionalism of the actors, technicians, and others that maintains productivity and discipline.

It is similar in a Dojo. The only obvious rewards that a Sensei can bestow are higher rank belts. One punishment appears to be withholding the privilege of grading or testing for a higher belt. The ultimate punishment is expulsion from the Dojo, which is reserved for major offences such as drug use or the unjustified use of Karate outside the Dojo.

In business a lot of attention is paid to the qualities that a leader needs to possess in order to motivate followers. But little attention is paid to the responsibilities of followers. In fact, at least one CEO was mocked in a published article for suggesting that every employee in his company was a leader. Not only is this structurally impossible, it shows little understanding of the need to be able to follow instructions, or to appreciate the concept of followership.

A humorous sign I've seen in some offices reads "lead, follow, or get out of the way". Leaders must use their qualities to deal with an endless variety of people, issues, problems and challenges. It does not seem logical that leadership can exist in a vacuum. But can followership be taught? Perhaps courses for executive secretaries feature followership curricula. If they still exist, they may be found in small, private business schools, or short community college courses, but do not seem to be part of university business curricula. However, followership is indeed taught in the Dojo.

The swift following of orders is a distinct feature of Karate training. A Sensei is the best qualified, outranks all students and must have a facility for teaching as well as people skills, if only for the business imperative of recruiting and retaining students. But the focus in the Dojo is on the behaviour of the students, not the Sensei. Students are expected to attend regularly. The norm is twice weekly for beginners, thrice for Black Belts and more often when preparing for a grading. There are rules about decorum, dress, and contributing to Dojo life. It is expected that practitioners assist others, follow orders and vigorously attempt to master technique. The motivation appears to come from within the student more than from the Sensei. The Sensei or senior Black Belts inform junior belts about matters of decorum, ritual, and etiquette.

The class size, presence of other instructors, and voluntary attendance means that the Sensei might not see a student for days or even weeks at a time. Self-motivation can be a result of many factors. Healthy, prudent fear of being injured or embarrassed keeps many students training alone when they cannot attend classes. In business the fear of losing your job may be an excellent motivator. Pride of accomplishment, desire to impress one's loved ones, and other factors may come into play as well.

The core value of followership teaches everyone in a Dojo to take orders. Those taking orders may be asked to reverse roles instantly and give orders to lower belts. A successful promotion is just the beginning of a new quest. Followership seems to be as much a cause of productivity as leadership, self-selection, or any other factor. It is interesting to think what the modern office might gain through more followership.

Joining and Training

Unlike office workers who are paid for their work, those being led in a Dojo begin by paying a fee for the privilege. They are rewarding their leader before receiving any benefit. Dojo work is hard. There is little or no socializing. Members are pressed by the Sensei to train diligently and attend regularly.

Participants are regularly asked to volunteer in a variety of ways. There are occasional Dojo clean-ups or moves in which all are expected to participate. Senior belts are asked to help a newcomer understand the protocol. The senior belt in a group leads some exercises, and demonstrates technique for the class. Mastery of technique and the philosophy behind technique is a prerequisite for teaching others.

Authority in a Dojo

Authority is a tricky aspect of the leadership question inside and outside the Dojo. From where does a leader obtain the authority to lead? Authority can be legal or rational, as in the case of the police or school principals. Authority can be charismatic, as in the case of the politician or football coach.

In fact, one of the most successful American football coaches has explored issues of leadership from behind a bench. But, even an unorthodox leader such as a football coach has rewards and punishments available to him that are unavailable to a Sensei. He can bench, fine, trade or promote players. But he also tries to harness something inside those he is leading by trying to appeal to the players' passion for achievement and winning.

Unlike a football coach, there is never any doubt that a Karate Sensei can perform all the tasks he is asking of his charges. A

Sensei is, by definition, the most proficient person in the room. Competence is an important leadership skill, but often ignored. Some notable CEOs can display a knowledge of their company's operation that is encyclopaedic—as is a Sensei's knowledge of eastern philosophy and the Martial Arts.

This expertise that a Sensei possesses quickly translates into a benefit for his charges. It is this benefit that is a great motivator for students. In the back of a student's mind over the years is the notion that the Sensei is in a constant process of saving the lives of practitioners by pushing students to be fit, avoid the ill-effects of age, cope with stress, avoid physical danger, and deal with physical attack as a last resort, if necessary. Gratitude quickly translates into a willingness to do what is asked.

This focus on life-saving and mastery raises the notion of the generic skills which a leader must possess. There may be leadership fitness in the same way that there is physical or mental fitness. Few people do sit-ups because sit-ups are a life skill that they will use in the future. Sit-ups are valuable because they aid in a variety of sports and recreation activities, and improve appearance. Moreover, general fitness is not just a goal in itself, but prepares the practitioner for unspecified challenges (running for a bus, wrestling with the grandchildren, and so on) at unspecified times in the future. Leaders may also need generic skills in order to face unspecified future challenges. This is especially true for political leaders.

In all types of leadership, these skills might include communication, literacy, numeracy, emotional intelligence, human resource abilities, and so on. Mastery of such leadership skills can save the corporate life of the leader in the future. Imparting these skills to a leader's direct reports and staff can save the corporate lives of those staff members in the future.

Class Beginnings

Very few people are late for a Dojo class. Shoes are neatly piled outside the door. Participants line up in belt (rank) order. The "Rei", or bow, marks the formal beginning of a Karate class. The bow to the Shoman is symbolic respect for the history of Karate and for the pictures of long-dead Senseis on the front wall. This ritual is followed by meditation, led by the Sensei or the most senior belt present. This ritual clears the mind and has valuable therapeutic physical effects. As one goes about normal working life, there are regular reminders of the many small and large benefits of Karate training. After the Rei, the Sensei designates the senior belt to lead the warm-up of twenty minutes of pre-arranged stretches and strength moves.

The Shrine or Shoman

In Japanese, "Shoman" simply means front. However, the front of a Dojo is more significant than the front of a lecture hall, just as the front of a church is more significant than the front of a classroom. In addition to the pictures of Senseis, the Shoman contains a large mirror, a sword, an incense burner, and other small items of significance. The mirror symbolizes self-reflection. The sword signifies the martial aspect of Dojo activities. The Shoman also contains the pictograph for compassion.

同情

Compassion is an important element in Martial Arts and leadership. Sensei frequently displays compassion even when exercising authority. Senior belts whose actions could be interpreted as being unnecessarily officious or lacking in care during their sparring and instruction may find the Sensei asking sympathetically about their personal circumstances or business. He is not justifying or excusing troubling behaviour, but trying to understand and explain it both to the offender and others.

Most people are likely to react to the shortcomings of others with derision, anger, and negativity. But Sensei advises that when one is operating at a very high level of proficiency, skills need to be tempered to keep actions in proper perspective. Without a sense of perspective and empathy for others, it is possible that Martial Arts skills could simply turn into gratuitous violence. In the business world, the leader without empathy can easily become a bully or bombast. Moreover, many of those being led simply cannot or do not want to perform at the high level that some leaders expect. There needs to be an accommodation for those followers through empathy.

Grading

A grading is a formal event at which the Sensei and senior Black Belts assemble to judge a student's progress before awarding that student with a higher belt. Black Belts must grade not only at their Dojo, but also at the governing body for Karate. In this case, it is the Classical Martial Arts Centre, or CMAC. This double-grading transmits the message to students that they are involved in a continuous process.

Before moving up to a Black Belt, brown belts must first

pass through an interim stage and grade for the Mudansha rank. "Mudansha" means "no rank person". As soon as one becomes a Mudansha, the group dynamics change. Much more is expected. Black Belts and Mudansha usually get together outside of the Dojo and outside of formal class times to work through exercises and talk through philosophy and history. In a discipline that has so much apparent competition to it, this fellowship is remarkable.

Cardio Coaching

As in any other physical activity, fitness is vital. I sought out a great cardio coach–a fit young man in his early 20s. He'd rowed for Upper Canada College, Ridley College and Trinity College at the University of Toronto. He subsequently rowed for Brasenose College at Oxford University. This very tough coach was my son, Oxonian, Michael Bonner, whose advice I'm paraphrasing below.

One of the first pieces of advice when using a rowing machine is to neutralize the face. If you grimace it uses up a small amount of energy that should be saved for moving the oars. The next piece of advice is to avoid looking at the machine's LED, which displays the elapsed time, strokes per minute and metres travelled. There is a tendency to be self-congratulatory if the numbers look good, or to speed up in order to make the numbers improve. But there are no numbers on a screen in an actual rowing event on the water, so the rower simply rows the best s/he can in order to win. The only feedback on the water is the feeling of exertion and the proximity of competitors' boats. So the only feedback one should use in training is the feeling of very hard work. Maintaining that feeling will produce the desired result. Looking at the numbers is a distraction.

In our workaday world it could be argued that many managers, regardless of occupation, do not really know what hard work is. But it can be highly motivational and satisfying to engage in very hard work. It is also enjoyable to summon up that feeling at a later date and replicate it. The feeling of hard work becomes a litmus test by which future efforts can be judged. Mental activity can produce a feeling of exhaustion similar to the one achieved through physical exercise.

The attention to bio-mechanical detail needed to succeed in a Dojo does not have a parallel in modern offices. There is no talk about the correct posture required for greater focus and concentration. I am aware of some discussion of ergonomics to deal with the avoidance of injury, and by extension, to increase productivity. But one hundred years of time and motion studies have not caused the shop floor or secretarial pool to have individual bio-mechanics in mind during a typical workday. If Dojo attitudes were prevalent in business life, there would be discussion about the most appropriate sitting posture to employ for telephone and computer use, reading, composing documents and so on.

Information of this kind may exist in medical literature, or obscure business publications, but that's all. Further, if Dojo attitudes prevailed in business, managers would be aware of the absolute necessity of arriving and ending on time, having an agenda, the assignment of tasks, and follow-up. There would also be commentary on the optimum posture, facial expressions, body language, gestures, and eye contact to use in a productive encounter with a co-worker. The above examples may sound a bit far fetched, but few Martial Artists, military officers, diplomats, trade officials, or elite athletes whom I've known and coached would question this focus on the details in order to achieve optimum performance.

If we extend the analogy, would modern executives be content to be hard at work the day after a major victory? A Martial Artist is expected in class for vigorous training the day after a Black Belt grading to show s/he is involved in a continuous process and that Black Belt is not the end. Would modern executives be satisfied with just knowing they had done a good job, or would they need the approval of others as proof? Would rank, title, privilege, and personal satisfaction be enough? Would executives want their family members seeing them perform at a business negotiation or closing in the same way that family members attend gradings?

One large oil company I've worked for has a relevant line in its ethics policy. It states that executives' activities should be justifiable to friends, media, and family members. Perhaps organizational life would benefit from lots of such outside scrutiny.

It might also benefit from the regular setting of large goals, and celebration of their attainment. Karate practitioners are motivated by small rewards and rank, and strive for the seniority in order to inject some of their own technique into Dojo activities.

For fear of leaving the impression that the intensity of Karate is the answer to the corporate ills of the last forty years, a note of caution is in order. First, the image of Karate as a macho activity with Dojos containing some unsavoury or sinister characters is not without foundation. There has been much progress in the past one hundred or so years, but there is a dark side to the history of the activity. Some Dojos in large American cities are tough places. Dojos in rural areas may not feature the spiritual elements and camaraderie that can be found in a sophisticated urban environment. So all is not perfection in Dojos. My experience is limited to two Dojos within the CMAC system over an 18-year period.

Moreover, no one can sustain the kind of activity described above. Nor could one sustain the administrative equivalent in an office. A workable methodology in business life might involve regular intense activity in the office, goal attainment, reward and return to slightly above-normal activity. Moreover, the intense activity could be rotated through the ranks, acting as a motivator for others whose intense activity would come later. In the end, the Karate metaphor may best illustrate the need for continuous and vigorous pursuit of tasks, skills, and the regular setting of new goals.

The Martial Aspects of Karate

The martial aspect of Karate may not be relevant or possible in Western egalitarian office settings, but the experience in the Dojo shows that discipline can be achieved in subtle ways. There is no macho behaviour or bullying, and very little harsh talk. The lining up, the bow, the uniform, and the configuration of the Dojo are all constantly reminding participants that they are involved in a structured, ancient, and effective system. In the same way that one cannot stop in the middle of a real battle, one never stops a kata–the detailed patterns of Karate movements practised either solo, in groups or in pairs. When in pairs there is real contact and the ritual is often called kumute.

Western corporations could be enriched by a little discipline, ritual, and the knowledge that the marketplace can be a dangerous place. In one generation of office workers, typewriters, certain types of telephones, telephone companies, and entire job descriptions have become obsolete. It is not hard to imagine voice recognition technology rendering keypads on telephones or even keyboards for computers obsolete. The long-awaited convergence of telephones, television sets, computers and such will have profound effects on telephone companies, broadcasters, the practice of medicine, movie theatres, and perhaps many other businesses. Perhaps some healthy fear of becoming redundant in the near future would motivate R & D, customer service, sales, and other departments.

There may be a place for more ritual in modern offices too. Perhaps North American offices would benefit from rituals that stipulate that each day begin on time with small goals being set for each day. Ritual might lessen ersatz work, miscommunication, and lost documents.

Regimental history is an important source of pride and education in Western armies. Recruits develop a source of pride and duty by learning that they are part of a larger, historical context than the immediate task or situation at hand. Many formal lectures are mandatory. Some regiments have museums, and most have memorabilia in mess halls or in safe keeping. A civilian user of a mess hall notices the ritual and memorabilia, not unlike similar manifestations in the Dojo. Modern corporations might benefit from familiarizing new employees with past successes and failures and instilling a sense of history and pride.

Teamwork

A problem with the word "teamwork" is that it is as ill-defined as the word leadership. For some, teamwork may be a euphemism for the fact that everyone must work harder. It may mean more decorum or politeness for others. For some, teamwork may simply mean "do as I say". Few of those using the word team may pause to consider that much valuable and productive work is done by individuals. The Bletchley Park geniuses who cracked the Enigma code in World War II were probably not a team, but a collection of eccentric individuals. One sales manager with whom I was working cited the need for teamwork. When asked if he really meant some form of effort that an individual or a group could not make, he conceded that teamwork was just an expression. What was really required in this life insurance company was a number of individuals going out to meet customers separately and achieving group and individual goals.

In a Dojo, it may appear that teamwork is in evidence since all students do the warm-up and basics together. But this is really more of a group activity. Kata appear to require teamwork. But two or more Karate practitioners from different Dojos, who have never done a particular kata together, may look as if they are a well-oiled machine, or a team, when in fact they may simply be performing as individuals while performing with other individuals. This is a testimony to skills mastery and individual effort. It is only after years of skills mastery, alongside other practitioners, that teamwork emerges. It appears that team spirit must be earned.

Karate-Do

In Japan in the 1920s, the suffix "Do" was added to the word Karate to signify that it is not just a sport, fitness or club activity, but rather a way of life in which the spiritual and mental aspects are just as important as the physical. Many Karate practitioners exhibit a confidence in body language, facial expressions and speech that could be mistaken for a lack of humility. But the fellowship, support, and dedication to mutual success is palpable. The competitiveness and bombast that the author has witnessed in modern offices is virtually unknown in the Dojo.

If humility is manifested by helping others, having patience with those less capable, sharing proprietary information, and so on, then there is ample evidence of humility in a Dojo. Business studies contain references to the value of mentoring, coaching, teaching, supporting others, the value of shared experiences, and so on. All of this is normal and unremarkable behaviour in a Dojo.

Physical Learning

Scientific evidence points to a link between the mental and the physical. Exercise can reduce depression. The neuro-peptides produced in the brain travel through the body and attach to receptors in individual cells. Thoughts of fear or anger will produce a certain type of peptide. As they attach to cells throughout the body, the effects are harmful. Conversely, a positive outlook and experience create the opposite effect throughout the body, even to the point of preventing disease.

Heightened activity in the Dojo may be linked to two positive outcomes. First, the activity may create new synaptic pathways that can be used in all aspects of life, including business and family activities. Just as physical fitness prepares a body for a variety of activities, mental fitness can prepare the mind for different challenges. Second, the constant focus on the positive and the art of the possible in a Dojo may engender salutary effects throughout the body. Positive body language, facial expressions, posture and attitude may manifest themselves at the cellular and all other levels.

It may seem ironic that a martial activity, and one that ultimately deals in killing, could have such positive effects. However, the first rule of Karate is "do not be there", with *there* being the locus of trouble or danger. The second rule is to run. The third rule involves a parable from the East, which states that "when a lion and a tiger fight, one is bound to be killed, and the other badly injured". These rules, coupled with the notion of compassion, put the apparently violent aspects of Karate into perspective. The ritual bowing and compartmentalization of activities is also an object lesson that violence must be controlled.

It seems to be the intellectual and spiritual aspects of Karate that set the activity apart. With the possible exception of boxing, which has evolved into a controlled and relatively safe activity, there is not much at stake in sports when they are compared with a martial activity. The combination of the search for meaning, martial aspect, ritual, compassion, and regimental history may be what sets Karate apart.

It is easy to imagine the benefits in an office setting of positive outlooks, body language, facial expressions, and so on. These might counter the common complaint that the author hears that modern office work is boring. The "can-do" atmosphere of the Dojo might also bear fruit in the office. Perhaps transferring Dojo norms to the office would be difficult, but it is appealing to think of the effects of an energized workforce, grateful for the mental, physical, spiritual, and monetary benefits of office activities.

The Emergent Leader

In any given class, the Dojo may contain at least three small groups working on different kata, basic moves or other matters. A few may be working at mirrors to learn new moves through self-examination. Another group may be in a nearby room performing falls and take-downs on mats. Events move quickly. The shortest kata takes twelve seconds and the longest under two minutes. At any moment a student may move from being a participant in a kata that s/he is learning from a senior belt, to leading a group in a kata s/he has known for years. A student may also be called out of these groups to work with a new student on particular moves at the mirrors, or on the mats. The concept here is that of the emergent leader, or what might be called the ephemeral, episodic nature of leadership, which can emerge from within a group. But the fact that everyone can be a leader at certain times is consistent with both the literature and the Dojo experience.

Having Leadership Thrust Upon One

Positions of leadership are not necessarily prized. Hollywood movies feature story lines where an enlisted man wishes to stay with his colleagues in the ranks, and avoid promotion in the military. Some industrial workers may enjoy predictable shifts and the benefits of union membership over promotion. Some may even practise creative incompetence to avoid being promoted above their abilities. Yet, there is something special about a promotion: increased authority, rank, and the other trappings of office. So leadership may be a mixed blessing.

In the Dojo context, there is something very special about being presented with a Black Belt. There is the mystique of Karate and the trappings of office. A Black Belt is called *Mister* if a man and *Miss* or *Ms* if a woman. The deference is of course to the rank and uniform, and there is a poignant feeling of responsibility that comes with the new Black Belt. As a teacher s/he will be asked the meaning or history of kata. Questions will also arise about exact technique. The need to be an authority on skills is palpable. The mere act of wearing the Black Belt makes a difference.

Followers need to adjust to the style of their new leaders. Leaders need to adjust their styles to suit the activities or personalities of their followers. But the Dojo experience suggests that there should be more attention paid to the adjustments that leaders must make for their new roles. It may be wrongly assumed that leaders simply advance seamlessly to their new positions. There may actually be considerable discomfort, something I have noted in several new executives. No matter how suitable a candidate's resume appears to be, assumption of new leadership responsibilities may be wrenching. However suitable a leader is to the role, s/he probably needs to step aside regularly to allow for others to lead temporarily. S/he must also create a system that develops new, permanent, or temporary leaders.

The respect for office, rank, and authority may simply not be possible in modern, egalitarian, Western society. However, Western corporations might benefit from more respect for offices.

One wonders whether Western corporate leaders have earned respect. Dojo classes end with students loudly reciting a phrase in Japanese that means "Thank you for exhausting yourself to teach us". It is doubtful that Western corporate leaders habitually display the selflessness or valuable lessons that this phrase implies, or whether workers are selfless enough to be so thankful.

Decision Making

Quality decision-making is widely recognized as a necessary component of effective leadership. Effective decision-making is also an important feature of managing rapidly evolving situations. On first glance, there seem to be no decisions of substance being made in the Dojo. The Sensei instructs participants in techniques which they perform repeatedly. There seem to be no decisions that transcend the mundane. Activities, the uniform, protocol, and logistics are all prescribed.

The major decision is to join the Dojo. After that, other actions and decisions flow naturally, including the mundane ones about which classes to attend. Sensei decides whether a student can grade. That decision is primarily made as a result of the objective, demonstrable skill, and the readiness of the student.

There even appears to be a physiological and psychological approach in Karate that obviates decision-making. The practitioner does not want the brain engaged when Martial Arts skills are required in a real situation. Martial artists want muscle memory to be engaged, not logical thought progressions. This involves even less analytical thinking or thinking of any kind, than the naturalistic decision making (NDM) described earlier in this book.

However, there are several ways in which decision-making could be viewed as central to the Dojo experience. The decision to attend is a major one, reaffirmed each day that one trains. Because Karate-Do has a spiritual and mental aspect, this single decision has profound implications. It is as profound to the individual as a value, vision, or mission statement is to a corporation. The corporate decision-making process that arrives at such a statement and reaffirms it is not trivial. Neither should the individual's decision to engage in Karate training. Moreover, the commitment to values or to a way of life becomes a worldview or heuristic. With a heuristic as a prism through which to view events, the decisions that those events require are narrowed to a short list, and the need for some decisions is obviated completely.

If a corporate or personal decision creates efficiency in future decision-making processes, that initial decision is an important and valuable one. If that first decision eliminates dozens of future, small decisions, perhaps that decision has more weight and value than the cumulative future decisions. Certainly there is a saving of time. The one decision made and then followed should not be downgraded in comparison to countless future, inefficient decisions. Quality, not quantity, should be part of the criteria of evaluating decisions.

The second area in which decision-making may be central to the Dojo experience involves the acquisition of skills that may be required for future events. The basics, the kata, and the combinations that are practised are rigid, set pieces–many of which have not changed in hundreds of years. It seems strange to assume that a mugging might develop to correspond to set movements practised in the Dojo: low block, high block, middle punch, footstomp. This seems as unlikely as a bridge player deciding, before the cards are dealt, to play the three of clubs on the third round.

However, a Karate student is actually planning for every eventuality that could be faced in a physically threatening situation. This approach is not as unusual in life or in business as it might initially appear. The planning department may use scenarios and models that will never unfold exactly in the way that they are envisaged, but that does not lessen their effectiveness, nor suggest that decision-making is not central to that planning process.

From one perspective, Karate practitioners can be thought of as being in a constant state of decision-making. The purpose of that process could be described as "the pre-making of future decisions". This may sound implausible, until one considers methodology in other disciplines. A legal, engineering, architectural, business, medical, or other professional education involves, in part, the study of cases, rules, and principles that help dictate future activities. One might even suggest that the lawyer reading a case, or the engineer studying bending moments, is obviating the need for certain decisions later. Similarly, an accountant need not ponder a decision about whether to examine trace documents during an audit, or require two signatures on a check, if those actions are prescribed in the Generally Accepted Accounting Principles.

Policy and procedure manuals and job descriptions lessen the number of, and need for, future decisions. The military concept of Standard Operating Procedures involves breaking complex tasks down into component, manageable mini-tasks, and even pre-assigns them. This might be more rightly called delegation, rather than pre-facto decision-making, but the result is fewer decisions.

Observations

I believe managers of today's high-pressure world of business and commerce could reinforce their leadership by learning from ritual of the kind found in the Dojo. By focusing minds on time, place and purpose, ritual may also aid concentration and productivity.

Today, many workers appear to strive for a seamless work life in which digital technology keeps them connected to others at all times. The Dojo experience involves having a distinct beginning and end to work, to achieve greater focus. It also encourages quiet time or meditation. There may be a significant business value in encouraging workers to "unplug" themselves occasionally.

Demonstrating a skill is an important leadership tool, certainly as important as explaining a skill or writing about one. In addition to trying to master the demonstration of skills, business leaders might consider the value of much shorter time frames for tasks.

Rewards can play an important role in the modern office but not all rewards have to be corner offices, stock options, and cars. The Dojo shows that small, symbolic rewards can motivate as well. There are also what will become traditions that can be established in a work setting. These may include anniversary parties, outside social events, or running office jokes.

Group dynamics can benefit by taking a leaf from Dojo activities. These include:

- Success in working with a diverse work group in an increasingly multicultural and global society

- Leadership as ephemeral and episodic

- The emergent leader who comes out of, or is called out of, the group

- The idea of the led deriving benefit from being led

- The spiritual, and being of service to others in order to harness inner strengths.

Perhaps the major lesson that can be learned from the Dojo experience is that change and motivation occur within the individual. Leaders can create a motivational environment. Money and rank are helpful. But ultimately, it is something within the individual that must trigger productivity and commitment. A Karate Sensei cannot perform a kata for a student. A sales manager cannot visit all customers with his sales force members. A leader can instruct, but the doing must come from the individual. Money will not replace expertise. Sensei cannot pay a student to learn.

Few, if any, business studies have dealt with the idea that fear, ego, or embarrassment may be excellent motivators. Healthy fears–of failure, embarrassment, or not being able to provide for one's family–are all but eschewed in the modern educational system and in business literature. Yet they are an integral part of the Dojo experience. And so is pride. But taking too much pride in a performance that is better than a colleague's is not encouraged in our offices or work-plants. Even less encouraged is taking pride in a colleague's performance that is better than ours. Egalitarianism has come to mean we're all the same and no one wants to be the "tall poppy", for in Australia, the saying goes that this is the one that's cut down.

Another lesson deals with ageing. In the Dojo it becomes

evident that older practitioners must develop different skills from those used in earlier years. Especially in sparring, it becomes evident to students in their forties or fifties that new strategies must be developed.

A related lesson is about injury–after all this is a book about wounded leaders. There's an expression in old-fashioned sports training–"no pain, no gain". This was used by coaches to illustrate the need for an athlete to push himself or herself in training to the point of pain. In Karate, we added something to the rhyme–"no pain, no gain, no brain". Our philosophy is to work around an injury, and injuries do happen. I've done push ups resting my foot with a broken toe over top of my good foot to continue to work my upper body when my toes wouldn't support my weight in a traditional push up stance. Many of my colleagues switched leads in sparring to protect an injured forearm or leg. We go easy on the jumping and spinning to protect the cartilage in the knees. I'd rest during sparring by grabbing my opponent and letting him carry a few dozen of my pounds for a while. In short, we don't allow wounds to impede our training. We do allow them to modify, but not to end the pursuit of our physical, mental and spiritual goals.

Finally, the Dojo helps us prepare for failure. That may seem a bit odd but the hard fact of life is that we all have to confront failure sometime. In business the emphasis is on success, new methods and increased productivity. But there will be failure. There will be business failure, limits to growth, and physical decline of individuals as we age. How we deal with those failures is the key–not that they will happen.

CONCLUSION

It's tempting to have a neat and tidy conclusion to a complex discussion. It's even more tempting to have a simple solution to an insoluble problem. There are enough business books available that feature lists of what to do and not to do. But while these lists may be generally helpful, they're like books of etiquette. They get you thinking in the right direction, but there's still a big difference between the meals I had with Prime Ministers and the one I had outside Kogelo, Kenya. Protocol was different.

How protocol and solutions differ was made plain to me recently in Kuwait City. For many years I've had the privilege of consulting to the International Atomic Energy Agency (IAEA). The IAEA and its Director-General Mohamed ElBaradei were jointly awarded the Nobel Peace Prize in 2005 for "efforts to prevent nuclear energy from being used for military purposes and to ensure that nuclear energy, for peaceful purposes, is used in the safest possible way."

As I was delivering my seminar on leadership, the sources of power, expectations, and so on, I raised the issue of leadership traits in the Arab world. A delegate put up a hand and told a story that has stuck with me. It was about a senior executive just transferred to Tripoli, Libya. He was getting settled in his new accommodation, his new job and life in a new city. But he was having trouble opening a bank account. His assistant couldn't get the job done. His status in his company didn't seem to help, nor did his company's name. He tried enlisting the help of his human resources department. All efforts seemed to go around in circles and this simple task was chewing up increasing amounts of time.

"I couldn't help overhearing you," said a young man who staffed the tea wagon in the office. Many senior people wouldn't have taken the time with the most junior person in the office, but this one apparently did. He confided his frustration in the young man, who immediately offered to assist. Having little to lose after his long ordeal the senior executive accepted the offer.

Soon afterwards the executive was surprised to hear from the young man pushing the tea wagon that the bank would be pleased to open an account for him. He promptly phoned the bank and found that was indeed the case. Asked how he'd accomplished the impossible, the young man replied, "The manager and I are from the same tribe."

This brief story is an object lesson in many things. One is obvious–the wisdom of the crowd. There may be expertise among people who appear to be your juniors. Another lesson is reverence for authority. Rank, the senior executive's title, the company's power and the HR department's expertise couldn't get the job done. The informal authority of tribalism did.

A version of this is the emergent leader. The senior executive tried leading, then got out of the way, so that the young man who wheeled around the tea wagon could emerge to get a job done. Lead, follow or get out of the way.

Then there's a lesson about ego. Maybe it's not the force of your personality and leadership track record that is infusing the office with energy and productivity. Maybe it's happenstance, the markets, the personalities of the troops or chemistry. Maybe you're actually in the way.

The thought that leadership in general or any kind of leadership trait is going to make every task easier and every person more productive makes leadership the proverbial hammer—with every problem looking like a nail.

The Harvard Business Review has documented many failures as well as success stories. It conducts interviews with famous CEOs. It helps perpetuate the cult of the CEO. But if you read and think between the lines, this might be the wrong focus. How good is business judgement these days, considering the remarkable failure of businesses and ethics? Look back at the composition of the Fortune 500 over a few decades. How many are still on the list? How long do even the best corporations last? Lee Iacocca was a star CEO but performed less well the more famous he became. As he wrote books, did commercials and toured the lecture circuit, Chrysler's performance suffered.

In fact there's little evidence that public prominence of "star" CEOs actually helps improve company performance or stock value. Stories about these stars may be fodder for "in-the-know" discussions of panels of analysts, financial journalists and others seen on television, but I wonder how much of this filters down to the average person with a retirement fund, purchasing decision to make or a few bucks to invest. If you are old enough you may remember Victor Kiam who liked Remington shavers so much he "bought the company." I thought it was a great ad, but preferred shaving with blades. When I was a youngster, before I needed to shave, I liked the Phillips floating head shavers because they had an ad featuring Santa Claus sliding down a snowy hill on one. I got one for my 16th birthday, but soon switched to blades. Leadership didn't come into the mix.

As I was studying leadership with Dr. Roy Damary, I asked him how many people could name more than five CEOs? He thought for a bit and conceded that few probably could. How can an unknown CEO affect buying decisions or even investment decisions?

There's the dark side of leadership–excesses, rants and bad decisions and there's also the dark side of tribalism. I grew up hearing my father ask people if they were from a certain county or town upon hearing their last name. When Canada had about a third the population it has now, he was usually right. This is a good parlour game and conversation starter, unless you decide you won't open a bank account for the person who is not from a particular town.

There is tribalism in religions, cultures and races, but also in professions, sectors and countries. While working for the team negotiating the North American Free Trade Agreement (NAFTA) I coined a term–the sector-state. I put forward that one sector (manufacturing, service, tourism) or a profession (law, engineering, medicine) might have more in common with people in that same sector or profession in a far off country, than they have in common with the members of their own country. This sounds sophisticated and international until you think that it's just another tribal connection that both includes some people and excludes others.

It's hard to transfer leadership principles across tribal lines. It's even harder with charisma, rationality, legal authority, power, democracy, laissez faire attitudes, visions, values and personal traits. What about intelligence? What kind of intelligence–IQ, emotional, gender, race?

So, how can an arbitrary list of three things a leader must always do and the four things s/he must never do work in such a complex environment? The answer is they can't. As I noted above, these lists were destined for failure anyway.

And what of the wisdom of the Chinese philosopher, handed down through the ages and referenced early in this book? Mencius noted that when we are "subdued by force" we don't submit in our minds, "but only because ... strength is inadequate". But, "[w]hen men are subdued by power in personality they are pleased to their very heart's core and do really submit". It's tough arguing with a long dead and revered Chinese philosopher, but I'd ask Mencius to define "power in personality". Is it in the eyes, facial expression, body language, tone of voice or good looks. What kind of man (or woman) is "pleased to their very heart's core" and for how long? And to what will they "really submit" and for how long? Upon examination, leadership is not an easy topic.

With several leadership traits and several leadership expectations among followers, the likelihood of alignment is very low–perhaps 1 in 32. Followers may be very susceptible to motivation by a certain type of leader, but also very unlikely to be matched up with the "right" kind of leader for them. Think of the myriad tasks facing a leader. What is the likelihood of a leader with certain traits having to face a task that happens to require those traits? What is the likelihood of that leader having instilled in followers the ability to address those same tasks?

A leader with certain attributes may have followers with certain expectations and both will face unforeseen tasks. They will come from different cultures, which may colour their views. So we must use deduction and reasoning to remove extraneous and distracting material to make sense of the situation. William of Ockham (1287–1347) put it more bluntly. Ockham's razor dictates that the simplest solution is best.

So let's remove from the discussion the ephemeral matters of leadership, followership and the distracting trump card of tribalism. In the new age of internationalism, globalism or multilateralism, it's the task we are left to deal with. The task could be opening a bank account or serving tea. Even running the HR department is a series of pedestrian tasks–recruitment, retention, reward, replacement. Of course, leadership might emerge. The tea man might hire others and run a catering business. Or his service on the bank account issue might catch the eye of the HR department. If not, there's nothing wrong with serving tea.

My late father spoke out on this regularly. At age 17 he was in the Merchant Marine ferrying aviation gas to eastern ports of Canada and Newfoundland. These were dangerous missions in waters infested with Nazi submarines. He told me he wasn't sure at the time that he understood the geopolitical issues of World War II other than that he was on the right side–King and country against a despot.

One reason he joined up was to avoid the embarrassment

he'd face if he hadn't. But once in, he focused on his task in the engine room. He knew that if the engines stopped working his ship, the ESSO tanker Norwood Park, would be a sitting duck for a torpedo. Survival depended on his keeping the engines going. This was pretty simple stuff. Ashore in later life he worked in refineries, mills and later the construction and leasing end of real estate development, where he assigned simple tasks–grease the gland, maintain pressure, clean the boilers.

As in the Dojo, the task is the focus. Followership is expected because that's the route to task completion. Leadership involves being the master of the tasks–the one who has gone before. A lot gets done in this way. What's wrong with having task completion–on time, well done, on budget–trump leadership, followership, tribalism and psychodrama? There is satisfaction in task completion. And in that satisfaction may come profits, new markets, better policy, and maybe occasional bursts of leadership which spur followers on to even greater task completion. I hope so.

Appendix 1

The following is inspired by successful 12 step programs to overcome addictions and excesses. These aren't really steps, but are 12 things that can be said, admitted to and done every day to get closer to health. Productivity will follow.

1. I am wounded

2. I have empathy for the wounded child within

3. Only I can comfort that child

4. It is unfair and impossible to expect others to comfort that child

5. I, not others, am the raw material with which I can work

6. Possessions, money, awards, degrees and other earthly things will not comfort that wounded child

7. Discussion of the wounded child is best done with a therapist, not with family members or co-workers

8. Each day I will call out the man that boy has grown into to act in a healthy way with family and co-workers

9. Each day I will have a simple, collegial interaction with a person or a small group

10. I will use my powers wisely and for good

11. I will not always succeed, but I will keep trying

12. I can succeed in health and without wounding others

Appendix 2

The table below codifies many of the unique behaviours in evidence in a Karate Dojo that may also benefit a Western organization. The first column lists the activity or behaviour; the second column suggests how these might manifest themselves in other organizational settings, and the third column lists some benefit(s) likely to accrue if they are adopted.

This list of potential benefits in the third column is not exhaustive, and there is much overlap. Almost every item could have contained reference to improved morale, productivity, adaptability, and so on. Many of these words are related. Thus, an attempt has been made to vary the benefits and seek new potential benefits, rather than repeat the obvious ones.

As in a Karate Dojo, it is the reader's own interpretation of this list that will give it meaning and relevance.

Dojo Etiquette, norm or dictum	Organizational Application	Benefit(s)
On time arrival	Meetings begin & end on time	Increased productivity, improved attitudes
Skill mastery	Literacy, numeracy, organizational data	Credibility of those with skills and knowledge, pride, motivation
Short bursts of intense work	Deadlines, games, races, rewards	Engagement, time-saving, less fear of large or new tasks
Courtesy	"Please", "thank you", positive body language, Emotional Intelligence	Less back-stabbing
Respect	Positive body language, possible use of honorifics	Less gratuitous questioning of authority
Arrive totally prepared: Gi washed, equipment in good order, etc.	Availability of pens, paper & the tools of the trade	Higher percentage of the workday spent working
Bow in	Sign in, cloak rooms, ritual at reception?	Focus, compartmentalization of work versus commuting or family time
Meditation	Quiet rooms, times or zones. Scheduled reflection	Concentration when working. Feeling that employer cares
Use of uniform	Ties, pens, pins, mugs, etc.	Limited, incremental collegiality; pride

Dojo Etiquette, norm or dictum	Organizational Application	Benefit(s)
Focus, concentration	Limited small talk, computer games & distractions	More competitive enterprises
100% personal responsibility	No blaming others	Less time wasted hiding or looking for scapegoats.
Fellowship	Supportive, positive, team-building behaviour	Increased recruitment and retention
Followership training	Following orders, completing tasks	Productivity, leadership
Spirituality	Not just The Golden Rule, but the parable of the talents & the juggler at the altar.	Fellowship, productivity and purpose, recruitment and retention
Teaching & giving back	Mentoring, coaching, modelling, partnering, Corporate Social Responsibility	Continuity, camaraderie, skills transfer, deeper knowledge in the teacher, better reputation in the community, among regulators and legislators
Fear of failure	Education of workers on market forces, competition & innovation	Motivation, productivity
Ego	Pride of accomplishment	More accomplishment
Respect for Authority	Followership	New, emergent leaders, bench strength

Dojo Etiquette, norm or dictum	Organizational Application	Benefit(s)
Simultaneous teaching & learning	Androgogy—delegation	Responsibility, deeper, lasting knowledge, just-in-case learning
Gratitude	Loyalty	Less turnover, increased effort, higher quality output
Ritual	Social gatherings, company recreation centres, sports leagues	Belonging, comfort, predictable behaviour
Earned membership in a special team	Emulation of candidates earning membership	Deeper effort, more cohesion, synergy, loyalty
Harnessing self-interest	Portable skills, self-improvement seminars, education on labour force needs	Creation of a learning institution, knowledge management, more valuable workforce
Rank	Coherence in the organizational chart and titles	Fewer conflicts, directions followed more quickly
Health, safety, fitness	Exercise rooms, diet & other support information	Less absenteeism, more productive home lives, less demand on health benefits
Rule #1—don't be there	Caution in expansion activities, research, avoidance of bad business deals	More job security, dividends & longer corporate life

Dojo Etiquette, norm or dictum	Organizational Application	Benefit(s)
Rule # 2—run	Less hubris when deals begin to go wrong. Ending failing business ventures earlier	Fewer losses
Rule #3—when a lion and a tiger fight, one will be killed, the other badly injured	Recognition of the dangers of corporate conflict	More care, research and due diligence, learning from other companies, cultures and times
Grading Tournaments, CMAC oversight	Mutual aid agreements, inter-company committees, industry associations	Additional depth, safety & access to knowledge, isomorphic learning
Incremental progress	Small assignments & promotions	Greater employee confidence & continuous progress
Coaching, Mentoring	Knowledge transfer, higher, faster learning curve for new employees & access to previous cases and lessons	Fewer errors and omissions, a sense of belonging and connection
Mandatory essay on the history of Karate	Regimental, or organizational history	Loyalty, belonging
Hard work	Goal setting & attainment by teams in short time frames. Muscle memory	Increased capacity to be called on when needed. Higher average daily productivity, increased self worth

Dojo Etiquette, norm or dictum	Organizational Application	Benefit(s)
Focus on hard work, not evaluation	Efforts rewarded, training for generic diligence, fostering of hard work as a goal in itself	More job satisfaction, less busy work, less down-time
Focus on details	Process protocols on files, phone messages, meetings, bring forward items, ergonomics	Structural soundness, stable systems and ultimately a focus on bigger items as details do not need attention
Goal-setting	Written daily, weekly, monthly, quarterly, annual and life goals	Concomitant, incremental goal attainment along the way to possible large goal attainment
Standards	Standard Operating Procedures, policy & procedure manuals	Predictability, time saving, new employee orientation, less supervision
Seeking order in chaos	Empowerment, personal responsibility	Consistent productivity regardless of circumstances, crisis preparedness
Controlled danger	Stronger, more adaptable employees through progressively greater challenges	More adaptable employees, suited for unforeseen challenges
Search for technique and meaning	Constant scrutiny of self and organization	Unforeseen payoffs and lessons in a learning culture, expansion of value-chain offerings

Dojo Etiquette, norm or dictum	Organizational Application	Benefit(s)
Teaching as a skill enhancer	Harnessing of stored knowledge in older and unique workers	Harnessing organizational knowledge, motivating both teacher and learner with teacher developing deeper knowledge
Solitary work as a skill enhancer	Clear task assignment, performance appraisal based on outcomes	Fewer layers of management, empowerment, trust
Task and person orientation, not technology driven	Reliance on interpersonal and phone contact, not e-mail and voice mail	Deeper, longer relations, clear communication, shorter project turnaround
The joy of learning	Libraries, book clubs, discussion groups	Continuous learning as a goal in itself, increased depth of knowledge & capabilities, including those brought in from workers' personal lives
New skills for older practitioners	Regular market, organizational and personal analysis	Better fit, adaptability, less obsolescence
New skills for new situations	Empathic design, anamatics (testing in real world situations)	Higher market acceptance of people, processes and products
The goal of learning, not winning	Continuous feedback, self, peer & leader evaluation, retreats	Serendipitous discoveries while continuously improving & adapting

Dojo Etiquette, norm or dictum	Organizational Application	Benefit(s)
Ease and fluidity increasing with age	Streamlining systems, eliminating layers of management, tighter deadlines, more tasks accomplished	Longer senior worker retention, harnessing of lifetime knowledge
Long focus on big goals, not short focus on small failures	Clear, concrete mission, vision, value statements, rewards for congruity	Empowerment, coherence, direction
Twelve-second katas	Twenty-minute letters, five-minute e-mails, 8-minute phone calls, definite start & end times for meetings, do-it-now culture	Less boredom, higher job satisfaction, less fear of new tasks
Small, measurable results	Drafting paragraphs in letters, annual reports, completing measurable portions of tasks well	Confidence, competence, quicker starts, less fear
Moving on to new tasks, not belabouring old ones	Five-minute feedback, memos to file, collation at performance appraisal time	Less down-time, an onward and upward culture
Fog of battle	Fog of business, acting on incomplete information, recognition of rapid change during tasks	Adaptability, continuous assessment of situations, lack of ownership of paths, freedom to change
Skills mastery leads to creativity	Codification of skills required in job or department, measurement of attainment	Freedom to adapt & modify skills after mastery, motivation to master to attain freedom

Dojo Etiquette, norm or dictum	Organizational Application	Benefit(s)
Quest for self-knowledge	Rewards for importing personal, outside knowledge, employee skills & knowledge inventory	Harnessing the wealth of outside knowledge and personal databases of workforce
Individual action versus teamwork	Office Signage—"If not you, why? If not now, why not? If not, why not?" "Is other input really needed?" "Take it as far as you can, then call on group or team help"	Action not discussion, shorter time lines, empowerment
Varying perception of time	Feedback on timing of some tasks versus perception of time	Faster action, more tasks undertaken late in the day, knowing they can be completed
The physicality of learning	Ergonomic studies, proscribed biomechanics for use of office machines, furniture and tasks	Fewer injuries, less absenteeism, more energy, efficiency
Focus on competence, not creativity	Standard Operating Procedures, codification of skills and tasks	Freeing up time to become creative; competence, confidence
Accepting chaos and disorder	Creation of a do-it-now culture, frank discussions of uncertainty, productive meeting without agendas	Adaptability, less decline in productivity in troubled times

Dojo Etiquette, norm or dictum	Organizational Application	Benefit(s)
Empathy	Individual empathy for self, radiating out to empathy for group and organization through frank discussions of work/life balance and market realities	Less anger & alienation of management from labour, divisions & co-workers
Family and other non-ego motivators	Family day at the office, personal stories and artefacts in the office	Harnessing of pride and ethics
Episodic, ephemeral leadership	Leadership from the middle of a group, hand offs to other leaders, development of leadership traits in all	Tapping into deep personal knowledge and skills within groups, adaptability
Student focus and responsibility	Emphasis on management team, quality of workers processes and technology	Cult of the worker and/or organization versus cult of the leader. Ease of transition to new leadership, looking to self for motivation, not leader
Sensei's superior skills	Leaders' demonstration of skills in training or other situations	Respect for authority, mutual empathy, deeper knowledge, faith in the system & leader
Continuous training at all levels	Leadership fitness in literacy, numeracy and tasks	Respect for authority, empathy for workers

Dojo Etiquette, norm or dictum	Organizational Application	Benefit(s)
Oos! (Japanese for "I understand and will vigorously and diligently pursue this goal.")	Positive attitudes, perseverance	Less down-time for angst and complaining
Feeling of hard work	High goal setting and attainment, followed by a return to normal productivity	Eventual elevation of normal productivity levels
Acceptance of the inevitability of errors and omissions	Focus on big goals, not small problems along the way	Less down-time for commiserating
Relaxation during sparring	Focus on solutions not problems	Clearer heads during crises & challenges
Task and time focus	Foreshortening of time frames & goal attainment	Less ersatz work
Zen is now	Being in the moment with a person or task	Respect, focus, purpose
Solar plexus learning	Drills, simulations	Safe & varied organizational reflexes
Kata	Fire drills	Safe egress
Decision to join trumping all others	Ethics statement	Confidence, due diligence, protection from legal offences

Dojo Etiquette, norm or dictum	Organizational Application	Benefit(s)
Late arrives ahead	Best practices, benchmarking	Continuous catch up, Commoditization
Ahead	Developing USPs (Unique Selling Proposition)	Differentiation
Decision to join trumping all others	Ethics statement	Confidence, due diligence, protection from legal offences
Ahead of ahead	Strategic planning	Corporate flourishing
Muscle memory	Standard Operating Procedures	Fast action, fewer meetings, tasks characterized as technical fixes & standards, not objectives
Insignia	Pins, pens, mugs, ties	Belonging
Personal quest	Just–in–case learning	Deep knowledge, preparedness
Sensei teaching one student specific and different techniques in a kata	Psychometrics, modification of job descriptions to match candidates' skills	Fast action where it is needed, deliberation where that is appropriate

Appendix 3

A Summary of Insights

Leaders exhibit as much work avoidance and busy work as any worker.

Leaders have psychological flaws that manifest themselves in personal and professional life.

Leaders have a tendency to harm those around them and even their organizations with their hard-driving styles.

Leaders lack basic skills in literacy and numeracy.

Leaders do not do their homework.

Generations of North American leaders have been spoiled by seemingly limitless growth through resource-sector exploitation, immigration, and inflation.

One of the most difficult things in personal and professional life is to be fully present and accounted for, physically, mentally, and psychologically.

Ritual can foster focus.

Modern organizations are too complex for senior management to understand fully or manage effectively.

There are limits to biological, organizational, and individual growth.

Certain management skills and decision-making techniques that serve organizations well in normal times may make matters worse in crises or other unusual situations.

There are different thinking and decision-making styles that should be used in unusual business circumstances.

The assumption that all employees want to take on more responsibility is incorrect.

Many employees wish to achieve their potential or self-actualize outside business hours with family, friends, or non-work related activities.

All people need down-time and reflection.

The modern office does not encourage down-time and reflection.

Modern business life and the wired, plugged-in regimes discourage down-time and reflection.

Modern communication devices may not actually increase productivity in all cases.

Modern communication devices may not be needed or effectively used by many employees.

Fellowship, spirituality, and camaraderie can enhance productivity and well-being.

Basic leadership skills are essential for success.

Teaching and giving back to the organization or others is beneficial and vital for success.

Fear and ego are acceptable motivators, but great achievement requires more motivation than these can provide.

Leadership is episodic and ephemeral.

If there is leadership, there must be followership.

Followership is episodic and ephemeral, even for leaders.

There should be more focus on workers and their contribution to organizational life, as opposed to the cult of leadership.

People at all levels quickly lose the gratitude they had when they entered the workforce or company, or took the assignment.

Gratitude is an excellent motivator, and should be maintained.

Ritual can play a vital role in organizational life.

Teamwork is an overused cliché. Much productive work is done by individuals and groups.

Legitimate self-interest and the deriving of benefits is an acceptable motivator.

Rank and respect for authority can increase productivity.

Modern executives have a cavalier attitude toward their own health, the health of their colleagues, and even the health of their organizations. More attention to safety and health can increase productivity.

There is value in outside oversight of activities.

There is value in incremental progress.

There is value in having a qualified mentor or coach.

The skills that a leader may need for future events can be termed leadership fitness.

Leaders need just-in-case learning as much or more than just-in-time learning.

There is value in an organization preserving and promoting its history.

Most people are capable of much harder work than they think.

More work is possible when the focus is on working hard, not evaluating the work in progress.

There is productivity in focusing on the details of a work assignment.

Goal setting and perseverance increase productivity.

Standards increase productivity.

Seeking order out of chaos is an aspect of learning, productivity, and leadership.

Controlled danger or conflict can result in clarity and productivity.

Productivity is increased through a search for technique and meaning.

Teaching and solitary work both lead to increased mastery.

Much office technology is superfluous and does not add to productivity.

Taking full responsibility for one's actions increases productivity and well-being.

Learning and productivity should be joyous experiences.

Productivity can be enhanced with very short bursts of work.

Organizations do not learn well from each other, especially if the learning opportunity is separated by time, space, or culture.

Systems theory and isomorphic learning can enhance organizational learning and effectiveness.

Team membership must be earned, not bestowed or demanded.

Regular bursts of hard work, followed by a reward can be therapeutic and productive.

Leaders must develop new skills as they age.

Leaders must develop new skills for new situations.

Leaders must prepare for and face failure.

Leadership and management goals should be to learn continuously, not necessarily to win.

There should be, acquired with age, an ease and fluidity with work.

Leaders should have a long focus on big goals, not a short focus on small failures.

The number-one rule regarding danger should be *do not be there.*

The number-two rule regarding danger should be to *run*.

The number-three rule is that *when there is danger, there will probably be injury.*

Time is not well used by executives or organizations.

Leaders do not take full responsibility for their actions and organizations.

Small, measurable results can lead to surprisingly large outcomes.

Leaders and organizations repeatedly use outdated or ineffective techniques.

Leaders belabour points or activities unnecessarily.

Individual action is often more important than teamwork.

There is a fog of business just as there is a fog of battle.

Skills mastery is the route to creativity.

Leaders need more self-knowledge.

Leaders need downtime for reflection.

Time is perceived differently by different people in different circumstances.

There is a physical aspect to learning.

Creativity is over-rated, and competence is under-rated.

Seeking or demanding order and logic is not always productive.

Empathy is a vitally important element in leadership and success.

BIBLIOGRAPHY

Aiello, Robert and Michael D. Watkins, "The Fine Art of Friendly Acquisition", Harvard Business Review, November-December 2000, in Harvard Business Review on Mergers and Acquisitions. Boston: Harvard Business School Press, 2000.

Akass, Clive, "Dot.com: why the bubble burst", in Personal Computer World, July 7, 2003. http://www.vnunet.com/personal-computer-world/features/2045854/dot-com-why-bubble-burst (August 3, 2005).

Amabile, Teresa A., Constance N. Hadley and Steven J. Kramer, "Creativity under the Gun", Harvard Business Review, August 1, 2002, in Harvard Business Review on Innovative Enterprise. Boston: Harvard Business School Press, 2003.

American Psychiatric Association, Diagnostic and Statistical Manual of Mental Disorders. 4th ed, Washington DC: APA, 1994.

Argyris, Chris, Integrating the Individual and the Organization. New York: Wiley & Sons, 1966.

Argyris, Chris, "Interpersonal Barriers to Decision Making", in Harvard Business Review on Decision Making. Boston: Harvard Business School of Publishing Corporation, 2001, 59-95.

Argyris, Chris, "Skilled Incompetence", in Harvard Business Review. September-October, 1986.

Argyris, Chris, "Teaching Smart People How to Learn", in Harvard Business Review. May-June 1991.

Ashkenas, Ronald N. and Suzanne C. Francis, "Integration Managers", Harvard Business Review, November-December, 2000, in Harvard Business Review on Mergers and Acquisitions. Boston: Harvard Business School Press, 2001.

Ashkenas, Ronald N., Lawrence J. DeMonaco and Suzanne C. Francis, "Making the Deal Real: How GE Capital Integrates Acquisitions", Harvard Business Review, January-February, 1998, in Harvard Business Review on Mergers and Acquisitions. Boston: Harvard Business School Press, 2001.

Bakan, Joel, The Corporation The Pathological Pursuit of Profit and Power. London: Penguin, 2004.

Barber, James David, The Pulse of Politics. New York: W.W Norton & Company, 1980.

Barber, Scott, "Designing Performance Tests to Accurately Predict True User Experience". http://www.perftestplus.com/presentations/Perf_Design.pdf (August 3, 2005).

Beck, Ulrich, "From Industrial Society to the Risk Society: Questions of Survival, Social Structure and Ecological Enlightenment", in Theory, Culture & Society. Volume 9, London: Sage Publications, 1992.

Becker, H.S., (1966) "Introduction to The Jack Roller [by Clifford Shaw]", in Sociological Work, London: Allan Lane, 1971.

Becker, H.S., "Sociological Work: Method and Substance", 171, in Module 3, Unit 5 of SCSPO. Leicester: SCSPO, 1971.

Bertalanffy, L. von, General Systems Theory: Foundations, Development, Applications. New York: George Braziller, 1968.

Berton, Pierre, Vimy. Toronto: McClelland and Steward Limited, 1986.

Betts, Paul, "Self-made airline mogul with a taste of the high life", in Financial Times, July 14, 2005.

Bianco, Anthony, "Jack Welch: Fall of an Icon", in Business Week Online. September 13, 2002. http://www.businessweek.com/bwdaily/dnflash/sep2002/nf20020913_7795.htm (August 3, 2005).

Bianco, Anthony, William Symonds, Nanette Byrnes and David Polek, "The Rise and Fall of Dennis Kozlowski", in Business Week Online. December 23, 2002. http://businessweek.com/magazine/content/02_51/b3813001.htm (August 3, 2005).

Bierck, Richard, "The Language of Denial", Harvard Management Communication Letter. March, 2001, 6.

"The Big Spill", CNN, April 15, 1989.

Binney, G. et al, Making Total Quality Work: Lessons from Europe's Leading Companies. London: Economist Intelligence Unit, 1992.

Bishop, George F., Robert G. Meadow and Marilyn Jackson-Beeck, The Presidential Debates: Media, Electoral, and Policy Perspectives. New York: Praeger Publishers, 1980.

Bloom, Jonty, "Do mergers ever work?" from BBCNews. <http://news.bbc.co.uk/1/hi/business/607239.stm> (August 3, 2005).

Bolton, Patricia A. & Jon L. Olson, "Organizational Theory And Emergency Management: Can Risks From Industrial Hazards Be Contained?" International Sociological Association (ISA). 1990.

Bonner, Allan, Doing and Saying the Right Thing. Edmonton: Sextant Publishing, 2004(b).

Bonner, Allan, "Exxon Valdez Was the impact of the notorious oil spill overblown?" The Calgary Herald. March 19, 2004, A13 (c).

Bonner, Allan, "If You Are Managing a Crisis, Has Your Security System Failed?" MSc paper in Risk, Crisis and Disaster Management, Leicester University (unpublished).

Bonner, Allan, "Public Participation Is a Prerequisite of Effective Disaster Management". MSc paper in Risk, Crisis and Disaster Management, Leicester University (unpublished).

Bonner, Allan, "What Influence Might Cultural, Spatial and Temporal Distance Exert on our Capacity to Learn From Past Disasters?" MSc paper in risk, Crisis and Disaster Management, Leicester University, 1999 (unpublished).

Borodzicz, E.P., "Security and Risk: A Theoretical Approach to Managing Loss Prevention", International Journal of Risk Security and Crime Prevention. 1(2): 140-141, 1996.

Bramson, Robert M., Coping with Difficult People. New York: Dell Publishing, 1981.

Bradshaw, John, Homecoming, Reclaiming and Championing your Inner Child. New York: Bantam Books, 1992.

Brenneman, Greg, "Right Away and All at Once: How We Saved Continental", Harvard Business Review. September-October, 1998.

Bryman, A., and R.G. Burgess (Eds), Analysing Qualitative Data. London: Routledge, 1994.

Burns, Ken, The Civil War. PBS, 1990.

Byrne, John, Joann Muller and Wendy Zellner, "Inside McKinsey", Business Week Online. July 8, 2002. http://www.businessweek. com/magazine/content/02_27/b3790001.htm (August 3, 2005).

"Canada Red Cross tries to put blood scandal to rest", Reuters Foundation, Alert News. June 30, 2005. http://www.alertnet. org/thenews/newsdesk/N30536851.htm (August 3, 2005).

"Canada Red Cross uses HIV blood", BBCNews. May 31, 2005. http://news.bbc.co.uk/1/hi/world/americas/4595039.stm (August 3, 2005).

Cassidy, John, "GUT PUNCH: How great was Jack Welch?" The New Yorker. October 1, 2001.

Carey, Dennis, "Lessons from Master Acquirers: A CEO Roundtable on Making Mergers Succeed", Harvard Business Review, May-June 2000, in Harvard Business Review on Mergers and Acquisitions. Boston: Harvard Business School Press, 2001.

"Clashing with the CEO: What Directors Think-Special Issue 2003", from Corporate Board Member Magazine. http://www.boardmember.com/issues/ archive.pl?article_id=11779&V=1 (August 3, 2005).

Clement, Wallace, The Canadian Corporate Elite. Toronto: McClelland and Stewart Limited, 1975, 270-343.

Cliffe, Sarah, "Can This Merger Be Saved?" Harvard Business Review, May-June 2000, in Harvard Business Review on Mergers and Acquisitions. Boston: Harvard Business School Press, 2001.

Cohen, A.V., "Quantitative Risk Assessment and Decisions About Risk and Essential Input Into The Decision Process", in Accidents and Design: Contemporary Debates in Risk Management. London: UCL Press Ltd., 1996.

Collins, James C. and Jerry I. Porras, "Building Your Company's Vision", Harvard Business Review, September-October 1996, in Harvard Business Review on Change. Boston: Harvard Business School Press, 1998.

Collins, James C. and Jerry I. Porras, Built to Last: Successful Habits of Visionary Companies. New York: Harpers Business, 1994.

Collins, Jim, "Level Five Leadership: The Triumph of Humility and Fierce Resolve", Harvard Business Review. January, 2001.

Conner, Daryl R., Managing at the Speed of Change. New York: Villard Books, 1995.

"Corporate Responsibility", NewsBatch: Your Internet Guide to an Understanding of Policy Issues. June 2005. http://www.newsbatch.com/corp.htm (August 3, 2005).

Davidson, A., In the Wake of the Exxon Valdez. San Francisco: Sierra Club Books, 1990.

De Geus, Arie P., "Planning as Learning", Harvard Business Review, March 1, 1988, in Harvard Business Review on Managing Uncertainty. Boston: Harvard Business School Press, 1999.

Denzin, N.K., The Research Act in Sociology. Chicago: Aldine, 1970.

DePaulo, Lisa, "If You Knew Suzy…", New York Magazine, May 6, 2002. http:// newyorkmetro.com/nymetro/news/media/features/5976/index.htm (August 3, 2005).

Drucker, Peter F., "The Effective Decision", Harvard Business Review on Decision Making. Boston: Harvard Business School of Publishing Corporation, 2001, 1-19.

Drucker, Peter F., "Information Executives Truly Need", Harvard Business Review, January-February, 1995, in Harvard Business Review on Measuring Corporate Performance. Boston: Harvard Business School Press, 1998.

Drucker, Peter F., "Managing Oneself", Harvard Business Review, March-April, 1999, in Harvard Business Review. Boston: Harvard Business School Press, 1999.

Drucker, Peter F., "The Coming of the New Organization", Harvard Business Review, September, 1988, in Harvard Business Review on Knowledge Management. Boston: Harvard Business School Press, 1998.

Durschmied, Erik, The Weather Factor: How Nature Has Changed History. London: Hodder & Stoughton, 2000.

Dutta, Soumitra, and Arnoud DeMeyer, "Knowledge management at Arthur Anderson (Denmark): Building Assets in real time and virtual space", in Knowledge Management and Business Model Innovation. Edited by Malhotra, Yogesh, Hershey, PA: Idea Group Publishing, 2001, 284-401.

Eccles, Robert, Kersten Lanes and Thomas Wilson, "Are You Paying Too Much for That Acquisition?" Harvard Business Review, July-August, 1999, in Harvard Business Review on Mergers and Acquisitions. Boston: Harvard Business School Press, 2001.

Eccles, Robert G., "The Performance Measurement Manifesto", Harvard Business Review, January-February, 1991, in Harvard Business Review on Measuring Corporate Performance. Boston: Harvard Business School Press, 1998.

Etzioni, Amitai, "Humble Decision Making". Harvard Business Review on Decision Making. Boston: Harvard Business School of Publishing Corporation, 2001, 45-57.

Faraday, A. and K. Plummer, "Doing Life Histories", Sociological Review. 27(4), 1979, 773-92.

Feyerabend, P., Against Method: Outline of an Anarchistic Theory of Knowledge. New York: Free Press, 1975.

Fink, Steven, Crisis Management. Toronto: Prentice Hall, 1986.

Flesch, Rudolf, ed., The New Book of Unusual Quotations. New York: Harper & Row, 1966, 311.

Flin, R., Sitting in the Hot Seat. Chichester: John Wiley & Sons, 1996.

Franc, Helen M., (Introduction and Comments), An Invitation to See 125 Paintings From the Museum of Modern Art. New York: The Museum of Modern Art, 1973.

Frankel, Mark, "Spellbound", Turner Classic Movies. http://www. turnerclassicmovies.com/ThisMonth/Article/0,,82767,00.html (August 3, 2005).

Funakoshi, Gichin, Karate-Do-My Way of Life. New York: Kodansha International, 1975.

"Fuzzy Logic", Wikipedia: The Free Encyclopedia. http://en.wikipedia.org/wiki/Fuzzy_logic (August 3, 2005).

Gadiesh, Orit and James L. Gilbert, "Transforming Corner-Office Strategy into Frontline Action", Harvard Business Review, May 2001, in Harvard Business Review on Advances in Strategy. Boston: Harvard Business School Press, 2002.

Gallagher, Gary, W., The American Civil War. Chantilly, VA: The Teaching Company, 2000.

Garvin, David A., "Building a Learning Organization", Harvard Business Review, July 1, 1993, in Harvard Business Review on Knowledge Management. Boston: Harvard Business School Press, 1998.

Gates, Bill, "Remarks by Bill Gates, Microsoft Corporation, at Cambridge University", Microsoft. http://www.microsoft.com/billgates/speeches/cambridge.asp (August 3, 2005).

Giuliani, Rudolph W., Leadership. New York: Miramax Books, 2002.

Gladwell, Malcolm, "The Talent Myth", The New Yorker. July 22, 2002.

Goffee, Robert and Jones, Gareth, "Why Should Anyone Be Led by You?" Harvard Business Review, September-October, 2000, 62-70.

Golden, Dina and David Keil, "Interaction, Evolution, and Intelligence", http://www.cs.umb.edu/~dqg/papers/cec01.doc (August 3, 2005).

Goleman, Daniel, "What Makes a Leader?" Harvard Business Review, November-December, 1998, in Harvard Business Review on What Makes a Leader. Boston: Harvard Business School Publishing Corporation, 2001.

Gottschalk, Jack A., Crisis Response Inside Stories on Managing Image Under Siege. Detroit: Visible Ink Press, 1993.

Greenberg, Paul E., Ronald C. Kessler, Howard Birnbaum, Stephanie A. Leong, Sarah W. Lowe, Patricia A. Berlund, and Patricia K. Corey-Lisle, "The Economic Burden of Depression in the United States: How Did It Change Between 1990 and 2000?" Journal of Clinical Psychiatry. 64(12), December 2003, 1465-1475.

Gross, Jane, "A Dream Life Freud would have Envied", The New York Times. 7 November, 2004.

Grover, Ronald, "Fighting Back: The Resurgence of Social Activism", Business Week, (Industrial/Technology Edition). Number 3106, 1989, 34-35.

Gwyn, Richard, The Northern Magus. Toronto: McClelland & Stewart, 1980.

Halberstam, David, The Powers That Be. New York: Alfred A. Knopf, 1979.

Hamilton, P., The Administration of Corporate Security and Crime Prevention. 1(1), 1987, 11-19.

Hammersley, M., The Dilemma of Qualitative Method: Hebert Blumer and the Chicago Tradition. London: Routledge & Kegan Paul, 1990.

Hammond, John S., Ralph L. Keeney, and Howard Raiffa, "Even Swaps: A Rational Method for Making Trade-offs", in Harvard Business Review on Decision Making. Boston: Harvard Business School of Publishing Corporation, 2001, 21- 44.

Hammond, John S., Ralph L Keeney, and Howard Raiffa, "The Hidden Traps in Decision Making", in Harvard Business Review on Decision Making. Boston: Harvard Business School of Publishing Corporation, 2001, 143-167.

Harris, Thomas A., M.D., I'm OK-You're OK. New York: Avon Books, 1973.

Hastings, D., "Lincoln Electric's Harsh Lessons from International Expansion", Harvard Business Review, May-June, 1999, in Harvard Business Review on Crisis Management. Boston: Harvard Business School Press, 2000.

"The Hawthorne Effect–Mayo Studies Motivation: Elton Mayo's Hawthorne Studies", envision software, incorporated. http://www.envisionsoftware.com/articles/Hawthorne_Effect.html (August 3, 2005).

Hayashi, Alden M., "When to Trust Your Gut", in Harvard Business Review on Decision Making. Boston: Harvard Business School of Publishing Corporation, 2001, 169-187.

Heal, H. and G. Laycock, Situational Crime Prevention From Theory into Practice. London: Home Office, 1986.

Heifetz, Ronald A., Leadership Without Easy Answers. Cambridge, MA: The Belknap Press of Harvard University Press, 1994.

Heifetz, Ronald and Donald Laurie, "The Work of Leadership", Harvard Business Review, January-February, 1997, in Harvard Business Review on Leadership. Boston: Harvard Business School Press, 1998.

Heisenberg, W., "Recent Changes in the Foundations of Exact Science", in Philosophical Problems of Nuclear Science: Eight Lectures by Werner Heisenberg. Translated by F. C. Hayes. London: Faber and Faber, 1966. Based on Lectures originally given at the "Gesellschaft Deutscher Naturforscher und Aerzte", Hanover 17 September 1934.

Hill, Linda and Suzy Wetlaufer, "Leadership When There Is No One to Ask: An Interview with ENI's Franco Bernabe", Harvard Business Review. July-August, 1998.

Hodson, Kathryn S., "Does the Management of Crisis Suggest a Failure of Security?" MSc paper in Risk, Crisis and Disaster Management, Leicester University (unpublished).

Honour, Hugh and John Fleming, The Visual Arts: A History. 5th ed., New York: Harry N. Abrams, Inc., 1999.

Hyams, Joe, Zen in the Martial Arts. New York: Bantam Books, 1982.

Irvine, Robert B., When You are the Headline: Managing a Major News Story. Dow Jones Irwin (U.S.) & Toronto: Oxford University Press, 1987.

Johnson, G., "Managing Strategic Change: Strategy Culture in Action", in D. Faulkener and G. Johnson (eds.), The Challenge of Strategic Management. London: Kogan Page, 1992.

Jupp, V., Methods of Criminological Research. London: Routledge, 1993.

Kahneman, D. and A. Tversky, "Prospect Theory. An Analysis of Decision Making Under Risk", in Econometrica. 47(2), 1979.

Kaplan, Robert S. and David P. Norton, "Having Trouble with Your Strategy? Then Map It", Harvard Business Review, September-October, 2000, in Harvard Business Review on Advances in Strategy. Boston: Harvard Business School Press, 2002.

Kasperson, Roger E. et al, "The Social Amplification of Risk: A Conceptual Framework", in Society for Risk Analysis. 8(2), 8 January, 1988, 177-187.

Kellaway, Lucy, "Leaders of the bank unite", Financial Times. September 2, 2002.

Kierans, Eric W. and Walter Stewart, Wrong End of the Rainbow: The Collapse of Free Enterprise in Canada. Toronto: Harper & Collins, 1989.

Kim, Richard, The Classical Man. Hong Kong: Masters Publication, 1992.

Kim, W. Chan and Renee Mauborgne, "Value Innovation: The Strategic Logic of High Growth", Harvard Business Review, January-February, 1997, in Harvard Business Review on Strategies for Growth. Boston: Harvard Business School Press, 1998.

Klein, G., "A recognition-primed decision (RPD) model of rapid decision making", 1993, in G. Klein, J. Orasanu, R. Calderwood and C. Zsambok (eds), Decision Making in Action. New York: Ablex, cited in Flin, 1996.

Klein, G., "Naturalistic decision making: Individual and team training", Seminar presented at the Offshore Management Centre, Robert Gordon University, Aberdeen, March 1995, cited in Flin, 1996.

Kleiner, Art, and George Roth, "How to Make Experience your Company's Best Teacher", Harvard Business Review, September 1, 1997, in Harvard Business Review on Knowledge Management. Boston: Harvard Business School Press, 1998.

Kluback, W. and M. Weinbaum, "Dilthey's Philosophy of Existence: Introduction to Weltanschauungslehre". Translated essay. New York: Vision Press, 1957.

Kornfeld, Dr Jerry, David Meinz and Dr E Lee Rice, "Best Practices: Heart Health", from TEC: Chief Executives Working Together. http://www.teconline. com/www/bestpractices/heart_health.asp (August 3, 2005).

Kuhn, T.S., The Structure of Scientific Revolutions. 3rd ed, London: The University of Chicago Press, 1996.

Lagadec, P., Major Technical Risk: An Assessment of Industrial Disasters. Oxford: Pergamon Press, 1982.

Larkin, T.J. and Sandar Larkin, "Reaching and Changing Frontline Employees", Harvard Business Review, May-June, 1996, in Harvard Business Review on Effective Communication. Boston: Harvard Business School Press, 1999.

Lash, Scott, Bronislaw Szerszynski and Brian Wynne (eds), Risk, Environment & Modernity: Towards a New Ecology. London and Thousand Oaks California: Sage Publications, 1996.

Laverick, Tony, "How Can Systems Theory Contribute to Both Risk Prevention and Management?" MSc paper in Risk, Crisis and Disaster Management, Leicester University (unpublished).

Laverick, Tony, "If There Were a Theory of Security Would it Include a Theory of Risk?" MSc paper in Risk, Crisis and Disaster Management, Leicester University (unpublished).

Lerer, Seth, "The History of the English Language". Springfield, Virginia: The Teaching Company. 1998. Sound recording.

Liddell Hart, B.H., History of the Second World War. New York: G.P. Putnam's Sons, 1970.

Light, David, "Stock Who Goes, Who Stays?" Harvard Business Review, November-December, 1999, in Harvard Business Review on Mergers and Acquisitions. Boston: Harvard Business School Press, 2001.

Lipman-Blumen, Jean, The Allure of Toxic Leaders: Why We Follow Destructive Bosses and Corrupt Politicians–and How We Can Survive Them. New York: Oxford University Press, 2005.

Lissack, Michael, "Chaos and Complexity: What Does That Have to Do with Knowledge Management?" in Knowledge Management: Organization, Competence and Methodology. J. F. Schreinemakers (ed), Würzburg, Germany, Ergon Verlag, 1, 1996, 62-81.

Lissack, Michael R., "Knowledge Management Redux: Reframing a Consulting Fad into a Practical Tool", Emergence. 2 (6), Lawrence Erlbaum Associates, Inc., 2000.

Lovink, Geert, "After the Dotcom Crash" in Multitudes. January 2003. http://
multitudes.samizdat.net/article.php3?id_article=293 (August 3, 2005).

Low, Albert, Zen and Creative Management. New York: Anchor Books, Anchor
Press/Doubleday, 1976.

Lublin, JoAnn S. "Jail time doesn't bar pay for select group of CEOs", The Wall
Street Journal. March 3, 2005. http://www.post-gazette.com/pg/05062/465708.
stm (August 3, 2005).

Maccoby, Michael, "Narcissistic Leaders: The Incredible Pros, the Inevitable
Cons", Harvard Business Review, January-February 2000, in Harvard Business
Review on What Makes a Leader. Boston: Harvard Business School Press,
2004.

MacDonald, K. and C. Tipton, "Using Documents", in N. Gilbert (ed.)
Researching School Life. London: Sage, 1993.

MacIntyre, Alasdair, After Virtue: A Study in Moral Theory. London: Duckworth,
1982.

Maguire, John, "The Tears Inside the Stone: Reflections on the Ecology of Fear",
in Scott Lash, Bronislaw Szerszynski & Brian Wynne (eds.), Risk, Environment
& Modernity. London: Sage Publications, 1996.

Malachowski, Dan, and Kathie Lentz-Brockman, "Americans Waste More
Than 2 Hours a Day at Work, Costing Companies $759 Billion a Year,
According to Salary.com and America Online Survey". http://biz.yahoo.com/
bw/050711/115088.html?.v=1 (July 28, 2005).

Maletz, Mark C. and Nitin Nohria, "Managing in the Whitespace", Harvard
Business Review. Boston: Harvard Business School Publishing Corporation,
February, 2001.

Markides, Constantinos C., "To Diversify or Not to Diversify", Harvard Business
Review, November-December, 1997, in Harvard Business Review on Strategies
for Growth. Boston: Harvard Business School Press, 1998.

Marx, Karl, Capital. Volumes I, II, III, Sixth Printing, Moscow: Progress
Publishers, 1997.

Maslow, Abraham, The Maslow Business Reader. New York: Wiley, 2000.

Masters, Brooke, "What Does 25 Years Do? Stiff Sentences' Effect as Corporate
Fraud Deterrents Debated", The Washington Post. July 14, 2005, D01.
http://www.washingtonpost.com/wp-dyn/content/article/2005/07/13/
AR2005071302410.html (August 3, 2005).

Matthews, John, Healing the Wounded King: Soul Work and the Quest for the
Grail. Dorset, Great Britain: Element Books Limited, 1997.

Mayo, Elton, The Human Problems of an Industrial Civilization. New York: Macmillan, 1933.

McCaskey, Michael B., "The Hidden Messages Managers Send", Harvard Business Review, November-December,1979, in Harvard Business Review on Effective Communication. Boston: Harvard Business School Press, 1999.

McElroy, Mark W., "Second-Generation KM: A White Paper", Emergence. 2(3), Lawrence Erlbaum Associates, Inc., 2000, 90-100.

McGraw, Phillip C., Self Matters. New York: Simon & Schuster Source, 2001.

McKay, Bruce, "The CBC and The Public", Doctoral Dissertation. Institute for Communication Research, Stanford University, Stanford, 1976.

McLuhan, Marshall, Understanding Media. New York: Mentor, 1964.

McLuhan, Marshall and Eric McLuhan, Laws of Media: The New Science. Toronto: University of Toronto Press, 1988.

McNish, Jacquie and Shirley Won, "Rankin found guilty of illegal stock tipping", The Globe and Mail. B3, July 16, 2005.

Miller, A., The Drama of Being a Child: The Search for the True Self. London: Virago, 1987.

Miller, A., For Your Own Good: Hidden Cruelty in Child-Rearing and the Roots of Violence. New York: Farrar, Straus and Giroux, Inc., 1983.

Miller, A., Thou Shall Not Be Aware. Trans. Hildegarde and Hunter Hannum. New York: Meridian, 1990.

Montminy, Judith and John Lacey. "Millions of Americans Suffer from Major Depression: Only One Fifth Get Adequate Treatment, New Study Finds", News Release: Harvard Medical School Office of Public Affairs. June 18, 2003. http://www.hms.harvard.edu/news/releases/0603kessler.html (September 22, 2005).

Mouawad, Jad, "Settlement is Reached with Enron", The New York Times. B1, July 16, 2005.

Munk, Nina, Fools Rush In: Steve Case, Jerry Levin, and the Unmaking of AOL Time Warner. New York: Harper Business, 2004.

Ness, Joseph A. and Thomas G. Cucuzza, "Tapping the Full Potential of ABC", Harvard Business Review, July-August, 1995, in Harvard Business Review on Measuring Corporate Performance. Boston: Harvard Business School Press, 1998.

Newell,S., Robertson.M, Scarborough H., & Swan J. (2002), Managing Knowledge Work: Houndmills; Palgrave

Newman, Peter C., Renegade in Power: The Diefenbaker Years. Ottawa: Carleton University Press, 1973.

Nichols, Ralph G. and Leonard A. Stevens, "Listening to People", Harvard Business Review, September-October,1957, in Harvard Business Review on Effective Communication. Boston: Harvard Business School Press, 1999.

Nohria, Nitin and James Berkley, "Whatever Happened to the Take-Charge Manager?" Harvard Business Review, January 1994, in Harvard Business Review on Leadership. Boston: Harvard Business School Press, 1998.

Nonaka, Ikujiro, "The Knowledge-Creating Company", Harvard Business Review, November-December, 1991, in Harvard Business Review on Knowledge Management. Boston: Harvard Business School Press, 1998.

North, T.C., P. McCullagh, and Z.V. Tran, "Effect of exercise on depression", Exercise and Sport Sciences Reviews. Volume 18, 1990, 379-415.

O'Donnell, Jayne and Greg Farrell, "Business scandals prompt look into personal lives", in USA Today, November 5, 2004. http://www.usatoday.com/money/companies/management/2004-11-05-white-collar-sex_x.htm (August 3, 2005).

"Operations Management -Performance Management and Measurement", themanager.org. http://www.themanager.org/Knowledgebase/Operations/Performance.htm (August 3, 2005).

Parcells, Bill, "The Tough Work of Turning Around a Team", Harvard Business Review, November-December, 2000, in Harvard Business Review on Different Voice. Boston: Harvard Business School Press, 2000.

Pascale, Richard T., Mark Milleman and Linda Gioja, Surfing the Edge of Chaos: The Law of Nature and the New Laws of Business. New York: Crown Business Publishing, 2000.

Pauchant, Thierry C., Transforming the Crisis-Prone Organization: Preventing Individual, Organizational, and Environmental Tragedies. San Francisco: Jossey-Bass, 1992.

Pellegrinelli, Sergio, "Beyond management development: facilitating grounded, experiential learning", in Consulting Into the Future: The Key Skills. Karen Lee, ed., London: Hodder & Stoughton, 2002.

Pelling, Henry, Winston Churchill. New York: E.P. Dutton & Co., Inc., 1974.

Perina, Kaja, "When CEOs Self-Destruct", in Psychology Today, October 2, 2002. http://cms.psychologytoday.com/articles/pto-20021002-000021.html (August 3, 2005).

Perrow, Charles, Normal Accidents. New York: Basic Books, 1984.

Pert, Candace B., Molecules of Emotion: The Science Behind Mind-Body Medicine. New York: Scribner, 1997.

Peterman, J., "The Rise and Fall of the J. Peterman Co." Harvard Business Review, September-October, 1999, in Harvard Business Review on What Makes a Leader. Boston: Harvard Business School Press, 2001.

Peters, Tom, The Pursuit of Wow!: Every Person's Guide to Topsy Turvy Times. 1st ed. New York: Vintage Books, Division of Random House, Inc., 1994.

"Picking a Lawyer", Canadian Law Site. http://www.canadianlawsite.com/dealing-with-lawyers.htm (August 3, 2005).

Pidgeon, N.F., "The Psychology of Risk", in Module 1, Unit 3 of SCSPO, Leicester: SCSPO, 1992, 89-107.

Pidgeon, N.F., "Safety Culture and Risk Management in Organizations", Journal of Cross Cultural Psychology. 22(1), 1991, 129-140.

Pidgeon, N.F., "Technocracy, Democracy, Secrecy and Error", in C. Hood and D.K.C. Jones (eds) Accident and Design: Contemporary Debates in Risk Management. London: UCL Press, 1996.

Porter, John, The Vertical Mosaic: An Analysis of Social Class and Power in Canada. Toronto: University of Toronto Press, 1965.

Porter, M., "Second Hand Ethnography: Some Problems in Analysing a Feminist Project", in A. Bryman and R. G. Burgess (eds), Analysing Qualitative Data. London: Routledge, 1994, 67-88.

Prelli, L. J., A Rhetoric: Inventing Scientific Discourse. Columbia: University of South Carolina Press, 1989.

Prince, George M., "Creative Meetings through Power Sharing", Harvard Business Review, July 1, 1972, in Harvard Business Review on Effective Communication. Boston: Harvard Business School Press, 1999.

Rank, Hugh, "Watergate and the Language", first published in Language and Public Policy (NCTE, 1974). http://webserve.govst.edu/users/ghrank/Introduction/watergate.htm (August 3, 2005).

Rappaport, Alfred and Mark Sirower, "Stock or Cash? The Trade-offs for Buyers and Sellers in Mergers and Acquisitions", Harvard Business Review, November-December, 1999, in Harvard Business Review on Mergers and Acquisitions. Boston: Harvard Business School Press, 2001.

Rayport, Jeffrey F. and John J. Sviokla, "Exploiting the Virtual Value Chain", Harvard Business Review, November-December, 1995, in Harvard Business Review on Strategies for Growth. Boston: Harvard Business School Press, 1998.

Real, Terrence, I Don't Want to Talk About It: Overcoming the Secret Legacy of Male Depression. New York: Fireside, 1997.

Reuters, "Another Ally of Ousted CEO Purcell Leaves Morgan Stanley", National Post, FP6, July 16, 2005.

"Rising and falling with the economic tides–Fortune 500 companies", Nation's Business. October 1996. http://www.findarticles.com/p/articles/mi_m1154/is_n10_v84/ai_18732008 (August 3, 2005).

Robertson, J. (2003). "Where is the knowledge in a CMS?". [Blog] Column Two. Available at:http://www.steptwo.com.au/papers/kmc_wherek/index.html [Accessed 10 Jun. 2014].

Robinson, Daniel N., The Great Ideas of Psychology, The Teaching Company, Springfield, Virginia, 1997.

Rosen, Judith, "What They Do for Love", Publisher's Weekly. November 15, 2004. http://www.keepmedia.com/pubs/PublishersWeekly/2004/11/15/651077?extID=10026 (August 3, 2005).

Rosenthal, Raymond, ed., McLuhan: Pro & Con. Baltimore: Penguin Books Inc., 1969.

Rosensweig, Brahm, "Napoleon in Egypt", The Discovery Channel. http://www.exn.ca/napoleon/egypt.cfm (August 3, 2005).

Rowland, Wade, Greed, Inc. Toronto: Thomas Allen Publishers, 2005.

Royal Society, Risk: Analysis, Perception and Management. Royal Society Study Group, London: The Royal Society, 1992, 135-92.

"SafeWork: What is Workplace Stress?" International Labour Organization. http://www.ilo.org/public/english/protection/safework/stress/whatis.htm (August 3, 2005).

Sanderson, J., Criminology Textbook. London: HLT Publications, 1993.

Sawhney, Mohanbir and Deval Parikh, "Where Value Lives in a Networked World", Harvard Business Review. January 1, 2001.

Scales, Robert H., Yellow Smoke: The Future of Land Warfare for America's Military. New York: Rowman & Littlefield Publishers, Inc, 2003.

Schaffer, Robert H. and Harvey A. Thomson, "Successful Change Programs Begin with Results", Harvard Business Review, January-February 1992, in Harvard Business Review on Change. Boston: Harvard Business School Press, 1998, 199.

Schom, Alan, Napoleon Bonaparte. New York: Harper Perennial, 1997.

Schwartz, Tony, The Responsive Chord. New York: Anchor Press/Double Day, Garden City, 1974.

SCSPO, Distance Learning Study Notes, Modules 1-6 of MSc. in The Study of Risk, Crisis & Disaster Management. Leicester: Scarman Centre for the Study of Public Order, 1997.

Sellnow, Timothy L., "Scientific argument in organizational crisis communication: the case of Exxon (Exxon Corp.)", Argumentation and Advocacy, Summer, 1993, 30(1): 28(15).

"September 11, 1994: Suicidal Man Attempts to Crash Small Airplane into White House", Center for Cooperative Research. http://www.cooperativeresearch.org/context.jsp?item=a091194frankcorder (August 3, 2005).

Shakespeare, William, Hamlet. Toronto: New Penguin Publishing, 1996.

Shaw, G, R., Brown and P. Bromiley, "Strategic Stories: How 3M is Rewriting Business Planning", Harvard Business Review, May-June, 1998 in Harvard Business Review on Advances in Strategy. Boston: Harvard Business School Publishing Corporation, 2002.

Silver, Andrew and Eileen Morley, "A Film Director's Approach to Managing Creativity", Harvard Business Review. March 1, 1977.

Simons, Robert and Antonio Davila, "How High Is Your Return on Management?" Harvard Business Review, January-February, 1998, in Harvard Business Review on Measuring Corporate Performance. Boston: Harvard Business School Press, 1998.

Sinickas, Angela, "Communicating Is Not Optional", Harvard Management Communication Letter. June, 2001, 3-5.

Smith, Douglas Stephen, "How Can Theories of Risk Inform the Security Manager?" MSc paper in Risk, Crisis and Disaster Management, Leicester University (unpublished).

Stalk, George Jr., David K Pecaut and Benjamin Burnett, "Breaking Compromises, Breakaway Growth", Harvard Business Review, September-October, 1996, in Harvard Business Review on Strategies for Growth. Boston: Harvard Business School Press, 1998.

Stanton, Alex, "Management can keep a crisis from turning into a calamity", Oil and Gas Journal. 8 May 1989, 15-16.

Stettbacher, J. K., Making Sense of Suffering: The Healing Confrontation with Your Own Past. trans. S. Worrall, New York: Dalton, 1991.

Stryker, Perrin, "Can You Analyze This Problem?" Harvard Business Review on Decision Making. Boston: Harvard Business School of Publishing Corporation, 2001, 97-111.

Stryker, Perrin, "How to Analyze That Problem: Part II of a Management Exercise". Harvard Business Review on Decision Making. Boston: Harvard Business School of Publishing Corporation, 2001, 113-142.

Sull, Donald N., "Why Good Companies Go Bad", Harvard Business Review. July-August, 1999, 1-10.

"Supreme Court rejects patent on genetically-modified mouse", CBCNews. December 5, 2002. http://www.cbc.ca/stories/2002/12/05/scc_mouse021205 (August 3, 2005).

Susskind, Lawrence, & Patrick Field, Dealing with an Angry Public. New York: The Free Press, 1996.

Sutherland, E. H., The Professional Thief by a Professional Thief. Chicago: University of Chicago Press, 1973.

"T.R.: Theodore Roosevelt: 26th President of the United States of America", Biography of Theodore Roosevelt. http://www.theodore-roosevelt.com/trbio.html (August 3, 2005).

Taaffe, Gerald, "The Great Beer Scare", Maclean's Magazine. Toronto: August 20, 1966, 7-29.

Tanouye, Elyse, "Executive Suite can be Struck by Mental Illness", from The Wall Street Journal Executive Career Site. http://www.careerjournal.com/myc/survive/20010702-tanouye.html (August 3, 2005).

Thomas, W. I. and Znaniecki, F., The Polish Peasant in Europe and America. Chicago: University of Chicago Press, 1918-20.

Thompson, Clive, "PowerPoint Makes You Dumb", The New York Times Magazine. December 14, 2003.

Toffler, Alvin, Future Shock. New York: Random House, 1970.

Toft, B. and S. Reynolds, Learning from Disasters: A Management Approach. Guildford: Perpetuity Press, 1994.

Troy, Gil, See How They Ran: The Changing Role of the Presidential Candidate. New York: The Free Press, 1991.

Tuchman, Gaye, Making News. New York: Macmillan, The Free Press, 1978.

Waldman, Adelle, "A Prestigious Alma Mater Is Overrated on the Job", College Journal from The Wall Street Journal Online. http://www.collegejournal.com/successwork/onjob/20041116-waldman.html (August 3, 2005).

Waring, A.E., "Systems Methods for Managers–A practical Guide", in Module 1, Unit 5 of SPSCO. Leicester: SCSPO, 1989, 172.

Warrener, Don, Traditional Goju-Ryu Karate. Hong Kong: Masters Publication, 1992

Wente, Margaret, "Don't panic, but a stress epidemic is sweeping the land", The Globe and Mail. A17, May 17, 2005.

Wetlaufer, Suzy, "An Interview with Jacques Nasser", Harvard Business Review, March 1, 1999, in Harvard Business Review Interviews with CEOs. Boston: Harvard Business School Press, 1999.

Whyte, William Foote, Street Corner Society: The Social Structure of an Italian Slum. 4th ed., Chicago: University of Chicago Press, 1993.

Wilkinson, A., T. Redman and E. Snape, "The Problems of Quality Management– The View of Managers in Findings from an Institute of Management Survey", in Total Quality Management. 15(6), 1993, 397-404.

"William C. Durant, 1861-1947: Founder of General Motors", ClassicCar.com. http://www.classiccar.com/articles/william_durant.asp (August 3, 2005).

"William Henry Harrison", Answers.com. http://www.answers.com/topic/william-henry-harrison (August 3, 2005).

Wolff, Michael, "How to Get Away With Murder", Vanity Fair. New York: Conde Nast, August 2005, 92-97.

"Work-related stress", Health and Safety Executive. http://www.hse.gov.uk/stress/ (August 3, 2005).

"Working Yourself to Death: Stress on the Job", Facts of Life: Issue Briefings for Health Reporters. September 2003, from the Center for the Advancement of Health. http://www.cfah.org/factsoflife/vol8no9.cfm (August 3, 2005).

Wynne, Brian, "May the Sheep Safely Graze? A Reflective View of the Expert-Lay Knowledge Divide", in Lash, et al., Risk, Environment & Modernity: Towards a New Ecology. London, Thousand Oaks California: Sage Publications, 1996, 44-83.

Zaleznik, Abraham, "Managers and leaders are they different?" Harvard Business Review, March- April, 1992, in Harvard Business Review on Leadership. Boston: Harvard Business School Press, 1998.

Zeller, Tom, Jr., "Are Bloggers Setting the Agenda? It Depends on the Scandal", The New York Times. May 25, 2005, C5